Commander and Staff Guide to the Battlefield Coordination Detachment

Foreword

The battlefield coordination detachment (BCD) performs a critical function and role for the Army Service component command (ASCC). As an Army coordination detachment, and liaison to a designated air operations center (AOC), the BCD represents the Commander, Army forces (COMARFOR), while working in and among the Air Component Commander (ACC) staff in the AOC. The BCD facilitates the coordination between Army forces and the ACC, specifically between both headquarters.

The BCD becomes a vital link between Army forces and the air component by facilitating the integration and synchronization of air and Army ground operations within the operational area. The BCD is able to expedite information exchange through face-to-face coordination with joint air operations center (JAOC) divisions/teams, because BCD personnel are trained to operate in the JAOC environment using both Army systems and joint air command and control (C2) systems, and understand the operations process, joint C2 processes, and the air component processes (e.g., joint air tasking cycle).

A critical role of the BCD is to ensure the exchange of accurate and timely information, and to advocate for the COMARFOR as the liaison element between Service components. This role cannot be over-emphasized, as the BCD becomes the linchpin between Army forces and the air component.

The BCD also supervises ground liaison detachments (GLDs) and reconnaissance liaison detachments (RLDs). GLDs serve as the primary coordinating element between the supporting Air Force wing and the supported ground forces. RLDs perform a function similar to the GLDs, but with their focus on reconnaissance. The GLD's primary role is to provide liaison between the ground units requesting air support, and the Air Force fighter wings, bomber wings, airlift wings, and composite wings providing close air support (CAS), air interdiction (AI), airlift, and airdrops.

This handbook is designed to inform Army leaders of the BCD's functions, roles, and capabilities, along with best practices and lessons from numerous exercises, experiments, and named operations. These insights should prove invaluable to all Army leaders, newly assigned BCD personnel, and organizations that work with BCDs.

Stephen G. Smith
Brigadier General, U.S. Army
Commandant, U.S. Army Field Artillery School

Commander and Staff Guide to the Battlefield Coordination Detachment

Table of Contents

Center for Army Lessons Learned

Director	COL Michael J. Lawson
CALL Analyst	Mr. Donald Haus

The Center for Army Lessons Learned would like to recognize the following organizations and individuals for their contributions and assistance:

Mr. Anthony Gonzales, Army Multi-Domain Targeting Center

Mr. Karl Wendel, Fires Center of Excellence

Mr. Dan Elliott, Fires Center of Excellence Capabilities Development and Integration Directorate/Multi-Domain Battle

Mr. Sonny Clark and MAJ Steven Keil, Army Joint Support Team

Mr. Matt Neunswander, Curtis LeMay Center for Doctrine Development and Education (USAF liaison)

4th BCD Commander and staff (mission analysis/contributing authors)

3rd BCD-K LTC Bryan Jones, Deputy Commanding Officer; MAJ Howard Falls Jr., Deputy Plans Officer

5th BCD LTC Matthew Carl, Deputy Commanding Officer, U.S. Army Pacific

19th BCD LTC Matthew Arrol, Deputy Commanding Officer, U.S. Army Europe, Ramstein, Germany

251st BCD California Army National Guard

560th BCD and staff, Army Joint Support Team Commandant, Hurlburt Field, LTC Michael S. Willis

COL Yi Se Gwon, Director, Army Multi-Domain Targeting Center

COL Samuel J. Saine, Assistant Commandant, U.S. Army Field Artillery School

The Secretary of the Army has determined that the publication of this periodical is necessary in the transaction of the public business as required by law of the Department.

Unless otherwise stated, whenever the masculine or feminine gender is used, both are intended.

Note: Any publications (other than CALL publications) referenced in this product, such as ARs, ADPs, ADRPs, ATPs, FMs, and TMs, must be obtained through your pinpoint distribution system.

Cover Photo: Combined Air Operations Center (CAOC) at Al Udeid Air Base, Qatar, provides command and control of air power throughout Iraq, Syria, Afghanistan, and 17 other nations. The CAOC is comprised of a joint and coalition team that executes day-to-day combined air and space operations, and provides rapid reaction, positive control, coordination, and de-confliction of weapon systems. (U.S. Air Force photo by Tech. Sgt. Joshua Strang).

INTRODUCTION

"Liaison between forces is essential for coordinated and effective joint air operations. Component Commanders will exchange liaison elements to assist and coordinate the planning and execution of their component's operations with joint air operations. Liaison elements provide senior-level interface for air, land, maritime, and special operations forces (SOF). These elements consist of personnel who provide component planning and tasking expertise, coordination capabilities, and the ability to deconflict component operations and joint air operations." Joint Publication (JP) 3-30, Command and Control of Joint Air Operations.

ROLES OF THE BATTLEFIELD COORDINATION DETACHMENT (BCD): ARMY FORCES LIAISON AND COORDINATION DETACHMENT

The battlefield coordination detachment is the primary liaison from the Commander, Army forces (COMARFOR) to the joint air operations center (JAOC) or Air Component Commander (ACC). The BCD is a standing organization, assigned to an Army Service component command (ASCC), supporting a Geographic Combatant Commander (GCC), and located within the Air Force air operations center (AOC). The BCD coordinates both the Ground Maneuver Commander's plan and supporting air operations. It expedites information exchange through face-to-face coordination with JAOC divisions/teams, because the BCD personnel are trained to operate in the JAOC environment using both Army systems and joint air command and control (C2) systems, and understand the operations process, the joint C2 processes, and the air component processes (e.g., joint air tasking cycle). The BCD coordinates and receives objectives, guidance, and priorities from COMARFOR and staff. Specific missions include processing, monitoring, and interpreting the land battle situation, providing the necessary interface for the exchange of current intelligence and operational data, coordinating air and missile defense, and airspace coordination.

The BCD also supervises and exercises operational control (OPCON) of Army reconnaissance liaison detachments (RLDs) and Army ground liaison detachments (GLDs) that coordinate Army forces (ARFOR) requirements with supporting Air Force reconnaissance, fighter, and airlift wings. GLDs and RLDs are collocated at operational Air Force squadrons or wings. GLDs advise Air Force Commanders on Army organizations, ground force operations, tactics, capabilities, doctrine, and air support requirements.

1

BCD personnel work with their counterparts in the JAOC to facilitate planning, coordination, and execution of air-ground operations. The key functions executed by the BCD are:

- Representing the ARFOR Commander to the ACC in the AOC.

- Being an Army coordination detachment that acts as the senior liaison between the ARFOR and the ACC.

- Enabling selected operational functions:

    o Vital link between ground and air operations

    o Coordinating targets and all types of air support requests

    o Exchanging operational and intelligence information

    o Digitizing the Maneuver Control System/Theater Battle Management Core System interfaces

    o If the ARFOR Commander is also the Land Component Commander, may represent the Land Component Commander

- Facilitating battlefield synchronization in all areas of air support:

    o Air interdiction

    o Air Reconnaissance

    o Close Air Support

    o Cyber/Electronic Warfare

    o Theater Airlift

    o Personnel Recovery

    o Airspace Command and Control

    o Air and Missile Defense

- Exercising operational control of ground/reconnaissance liaison detachments assigned to Air Wings (fighter/bomber/airlife/intelligence, surveillance, and reconnaissance [ISR]) and carrier strike groups.

CRITICAL CAPABILITIES

The critical capability of the BCD is to enable human, technical, and procedural interoperability between all functions of the land and air component at the operational level in support of joint operations.

CRITICAL REQUIREMENTS

In order for the BCD to successfully accomplish its mission, it must first fulfill several crucial requirements. Regular direct interaction between the BCD Commander and the COMARFOR (or the Land Component Commander [LCC] if the COMARFOR is the LCC) is of foremost importance. This direct engagement enables Army mission command, by allowing the COMARFOR to effectively convey his intent to the Air Component Commander (ACC) via their liaison. This is the most basic element of human interoperability. The land component, extending from the Commander down into the ARFOR Staff, must regularly interact with the divisions of the BCD during both planning and execution. As a multifunctional liaison, this interaction is critical for the BCD across all warfighting functions of the LCC's staff, and across all planning and execution timeframes (e.g. G5, G35, and G33).

> **Note**: An observed common misconception is that the BCD's function is solely fires and targeting related; organizations that adopt this one-dimensional approach are generally challenged in their ability to achieve synergistic effects during joint operations.

The basic technical requirements for the BCD involve assured communications between the main command post of the LCC and the various divisions of the BCD, and the employment of common systems (generally Army mission command systems) to achieve situational understanding, pass mission critical data, and support decision making. The BCD's role as the technical link to the ACC's mission command systems (most commonly the theater battle management core system), implies a requirement that the detachment reside on the same network as the ACC, uninhibited by service specific fire walls. The final interoperability requirement involves the integration and participation of the detachment in Army, Air Force, and joint processes.

JOINT BACKGROUND

The BCD represents the ARFOR Commander to the ACC, so it is important to understand how the joint force headquarters will operate. The joint force commander (JFC) will usually assign either the ACC role or the Joint Force Air Component Commander (JFACC) responsibilities to the Component Commander who has both the majority of forces to be tasked and the ability to effectively plan, task, and control joint air operations. It is normally the air component command that supports the combatant command. The ACC will normally operate from an air operations center, joint air operations center, or combined arms operations center. The JAOC is structured to operate as a fully integrated command center and should be staffed by members of all participating components, including key staff positions, in order to fulfill the JFACC's responsibilities. The JFACC plans and tasks joint air operations within a responsive and integrated control system through the joint air operations plan (JAOP), air operations directive (AOD), air tasking order (ATO), and other guidance.

In addition to the JFC and staff, other Component Commanders and their staffs require continuous and ready access to the ACC and the ACC's staff. Principal means of accomplishing this access is through personal contact, an established communications and information support system, and liaison personnel. These liaisons work with both their respective commanders and the ACC and staff. Each Component Commander normally provides liaison elements that work within the JAOC, such as battlefield coordination detachments, special operations liaison elements, naval and amphibious liaison elements, Marine liaison elements, Air Force liaison elements, task force liaison officers, and others as appropriate (see Figure I-1). These liaison elements consist of personnel who provide planning and tasking expertise and coordination capabilities. They help integrate and coordinate their Commander's operations with joint air operations.

To promote understanding of the Commander's intent at both the sending and receiving headquarters (HQ), Commanders exchange liaison teams or individuals between higher, supporting, supported, and subordinate commands as required. Liaison officers (LNOs) working between supporting and supported Commanders are essential in determining needs and coordinating supporting actions. The LNOs help integrate their component's participation in joint operations, and coordinate and deconflict direct support air operations with joint air operations.

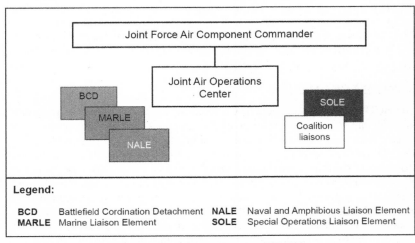

Figure I-1. Liaisons to the JFACC.

CHAPTER 1

The Battlefield Coordination Detachment: An Overview

INTRODUCTION

The battlefield coordination detachment (BCD) is an Army coordination detachment that acts as the senior liaison to enable selected operational functions between the Army forces (ARFOR) Commander and the Air Component Commander (ACC). Figure 1-1 (see page 7) depicts a typical BCD organizational structure. There is a BCD aligned within every designated Geographic Combatant Commander's (GCC's) air operations center (AOC) around the world. Normally, an AOC is a joint or multinational organization. The BCD is embedded into the appropriate division within the AOC, to ensure the Army Commander's needs are represented to the Air Component Commander.

Key tasks include:

- Exchanging current intelligence and operational data (priorities, friendly order of battle, scheme of maneuver)

- Support requirements (intelligence, surveillance and reconnaissance, joint fires, space effects, suppression of enemy air defense, electronic warfare)

- Coordinating ARFOR requirements for airspace coordinating measures (ACM) and fire support coordination measures (FSCM)

- Theater airlift

BCD MISSION

The critical role of the BCD is to ensure the exchange of information and to advocate for the ARFOR Commander as the liaison element between Service components.

The BCD represents the ARFOR Commander while working in and among the Joint Force Air Component Commander's (JFACC's) staff in the AOC. The Joint Force Commander's (JFC's) end state is achieved through the application of operational tools, to include the BCD's ability to handle mass volumes of information, and its leadership role as the ARFOR's liaison. As the ARFOR's liaison, the BCD staff must consistently understand and apply joint doctrine, understanding that there may be Service component doctrine differences with joint doctrine in the joint operations environment.

The BCD facilitates the integration between the ARFOR and the Joint Force Land Component Commander (JFLCC), specifically the integration between both headquarters.

Figure 1-1 shows how BCD sections plug into an AOC. The BCD's sections are spread across all five of the AOC's divisions, and work with the director of mobility forces, the director of space forces, and the director of cyber forces. The bottom portion of the diagram reflects how a BCD fully represents the COMARFOR (Or the Land Component Commander [LCC] if the COMARFOR is the LCC) equities, by plugging into those sections.

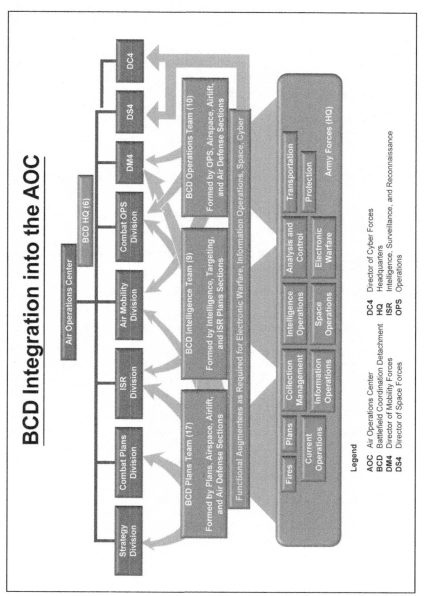

Figure 1-1. BCD Integration into the AOC.

7

The BCD staff clearly articulates the ARFOR Commander's requests for air operations in support of ground operations, in order to complement the Joint Forces Commander's end state. In this document, the ARFOR Commander is the Army command leading the Army land forces, and not the ARFOR with the reception, staging, onward movement, and integration mission. The BCD is an Army liaison. If the LCC or JFLCC is from another Service, the BCD would not automatically represent him. The BCD:

- Represents the ARFOR.

- May represent the JFLCC when requested, or if the ARFOR is the JFLCC.

- Exchanges operational and intelligence data between the JFACC and ARFOR.

- Relays and clarifies the actions of the land battle for the Air Component Commander.

- Manages the information to render a comprehensive common operational picture (COP).

- Processes the ARFOR prioritized air operations requests.

- Receives, submits, and advocates support for the ARFOR Commander's air support requests and target nominations.

- Processes air support requests (ASRs) (specifically ASR 1972s) in accordance with Combined Joint Force Land Component Commander (C/JFLCC) priorities, and builds air support lists.

While working among the JFACC's staff in the air operations center, the BCD represents the Army Forces Commander and, as necessary, other ground forces (combined, special operations, Marine Corps). As the ARFOR liaison, the BCD staff must simultaneously understand joint doctrine and apply Army doctrine, as the BCD facilitates the integration between the ARFOR and the JFACC, specifically between both headquarters.

The BCD takes an active role in the planning and execution of the air tasking order (ATO). The ATO is a product developed through the six-stage air tasking cycle seen in Figure 1-2. The air tasking cycle is a supporting component of the joint targeting cycle. (See Joint Publication [JP] 3-60, *Joint Targeting*, 28 September 2018 for additional information. CAC access required.)

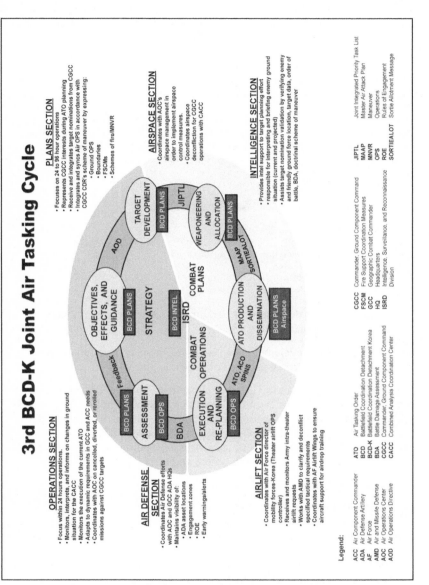

Figure 1-2. Example of joint air tasking cycle.

Figure 1-2 depicts where the joint air tasking cycle and the GCC can and should make inputs to the process. The conclusion of the GCC's mission analysis during the military decisionmaking process (MDMP) should provide the AOC with both mission analysis products, and the GCC's restated mission statement. This is a critical input for the AOC's strategy division in its writing of the air operations directive (AOD) for the United States Air Force (USAF).

A joint air tasking cycle is used to provide efficient and effective employment of the available joint air capabilities. Within the Joint Force Commander's intent, the cycle provides an iterative process for the planning, coordination, allocation, and tasking of joint air missions.

There are usually at least five joint ATOs at any given time:

- One (or more) being assessed for future action

- One in execution (today's plan)

- One in production (tomorrow's plan)

- One in the master air attack planning and target development (the day after tomorrow's plan)

- One in strategy development (examining objective and guidance for 72 hours and beyond)

The joint air tasking cycle begins with the JFC's air apportionment process and culminates with the assessment of previous missions.

The joint air tasking cycle stages are related to deliberate targeting. The approach is similar: a systematic process that matches available capabilities with targets to achieve operational objectives. However, they are not the same because joint targeting may be executed apart from the joint air tasking cycle and contains functions, processes, and procedures that are performed during peacetime, both before and after conflicts.

LIAISON TEAMS

Liaisons are an important aspect of joint force command and control. Liaison teams or individuals may be dispatched from higher to lower, lower to higher, laterally, or any combination of these. They represent the interests of the sending Commander to the receiving Commander, but can promote understanding of the Commander's intent at both the sending and receiving headquarters. Liaison teams or individuals should be assigned early in the planning stage of joint operations.[1] The BCD collates at the AOC and operates on a 24-hour basis.

Liaison support from the BCDs can include:

- Maintaining contact or communication between elements of military forces or other agencies to build mutual understanding and unity of purpose and action.[2]

- Establishing and maintaining close communications.

- Providing Commanders with relevant information, thus enhancing the Commander's situational understanding.

The U.S. Army-U.S. Air Force memorandum of agreement (MOA) for liaison support states: "Subject to the authority of the Combatant Commander, the U.S. Army will provide: A BCD as liaison to the air operations center and/or to the component designated by the Joint Force Commander to plan, coordinate, and de-conflict air operations. The BCDs will be assigned to the Army Service component command (ASCC) with duty at each numbered Air Force (AF) supporting a geographic combatant command." (See Appendix E on page 83)

JOINT OPERATIONS

Joint operations is a general term to describe military actions conducted by joint forces and those Service forces employed in specific command relationships with each other, which of themselves, do not establish joint forces.[3]

A GCC or JFC may establish multiple joint task forces (JTFs) within his area of responsibility. In these cases, a single joint force air component commander and joint air operation center may simultaneously support several JTFs. This option is known as a theater-wide JFACC.

In the event of multiple JTFs conducting concurrent operations, the ARFOR commander must establish priorities to allow the BCD to properly coordinate with the Air Component Commander, and ensure that the Air Component Commander support matches the ARFOR commander's priorities. The ARFOR commander may also need to reorganize the BCD to properly support the requirements of the multiple headquarters.

CORPS OPERATIONS

Large land forces require an intermediate echelon between the divisions that control brigade combat teams and the theater Army serving as the land component command. Other factors requiring an intermediate headquarters may include:

- Mission complexity

11

- Multinational participation

- Span of control

The BCD is unlike other service component liaisons because it is a formal organization with both a command structure and a standing relationship to the hosting component. Other service component liaisons are typically formed on an ad hoc basis, without the refined processes for coordination the BCD has established.

For additional information, utilize Field Manual (FM) 3-94, *Theater Army, Corps, and Division Operations*, dated April 2014, which provides the Army doctrine for the theater Army, corps, and division. It explains the organization of the theater Army, corps, and division headquarters, and their respective command posts. It establishes the roles for each headquarters, including their respective contributions to joint operations. It also discusses subordinate units and each headquarters' organization of its units, establishment of command and support relationships, and conduct of operations.

BCD FUNCTIONS

The BCD facilitates the synchronization of air support requirements for ARFOR or land component operations.

The BCD serves as the ARFOR representative in the AOC, ensuring that the Air Component Commander, AOC, and ground liaison detachments are aware of the following information:

- ARFOR intent

- Scheme of maneuver

- Concepts for application of ground, naval, and air assets in the ARFOR area of operations

- Enemy ground order of battle

The BCD operations and intelligence sections monitor and interpret the land battle for the Air Component Commander and AOC. The BCD passes the operational data and support data requirements of the Army forces to the ACC and participating multinational forces. These requirements include:

- Close air support

- Air interdiction (AI) target sets

- Information collection

- Joint suppression of enemy air defense

- Electronic warfare

- Airlift requirements

The BCD communicates the ARFOR Commander's decisions and interests to the Air Component Commander but the BCD headquarters element does not participate directly in the Army forces command estimate. The BCD provides requested information to the ARFOR headquarters during the command estimate and MDMP, and then the ARFOR Commander may delegate decision-making authority for specific events or situations to the BCD Commander. The ARFOR Commander clearly defines what authority is granted to expedite action on various functions supporting the JFC end state. The BCD assists with planning, coordination, and execution of the following functions:

- Intelligence

- Fires

- Airspace management

- Air and missile defense

- Airlift support

- Cyber electromagnetic activities

EXAMPLE

4th BCD Mission. The 4th BCD conducts liaison, integration, and coordination between the Coalition Forces Land Component Commander (CFLCC) and the Combined Force Air Component Commander (CFACC) to support land power requirements and synchronize air and ground operations within the United States Central Command (USCENTCOM) area of responsibility (AOR) and established combined-joint operating areas.

Note: The 4th BCD's mission is slightly different than other BCDs. The 4th BCD maintains a permanent presence, forward deployed in support of the CENTCOM AOR.

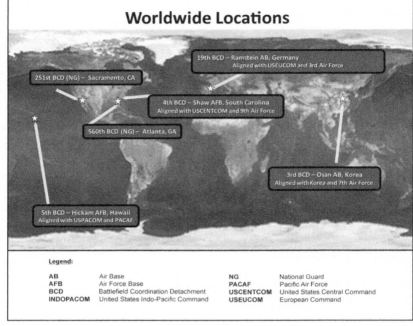

Figure 1-3. BCD worldwide locations.

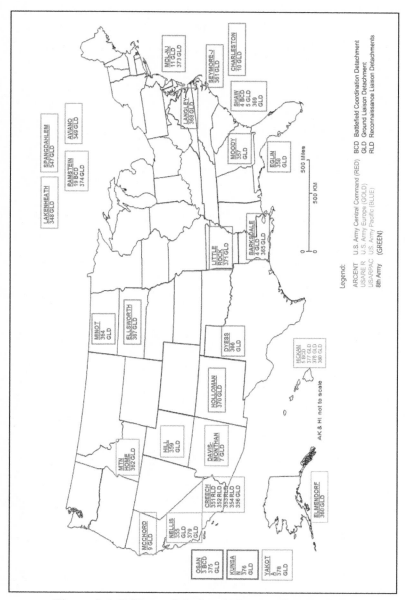

Figure 1-4. BCDs and their relation to aligned GLDs across the globe.

Endnotes

1. JP 3-0, *Joint Operations*, 17 JAN 2017, Incorporating Change 1, 22 OCT 2018.

2. JP 3-08, *Interorganizational Cooperation*, 12 OCT 2016, Validated 18 OCT 2017.

3. JP 3-0.

CHAPTER 2

Planning: Air Operations Center (AOC) Integration, Joint/Coalition Synchronization

PLANS SECTION FUNCTION

The battlefield coordination detachment (BCD) plans section consists of plans personnel who collocate with the AOC combat plans division. The plans section focuses on operations conducted 24 to 96 hours out, and performs two important functions. First, the section integrates and synchronizes air operations planning with the Army Forces (ARFOR) Commander's intent and scheme of maneuver. Second, the section ensures the ARFOR Commander's guidance and priorities are being used to enhance air support to the Army forces. Digital information systems support both the coordination of plans, and the rendering of a common operational picture (COP). The plans section also integrates Air Component Commander (ACC) requirements with the ARFOR requirements for information collection, military information support operations, and electronic warfare.[1]

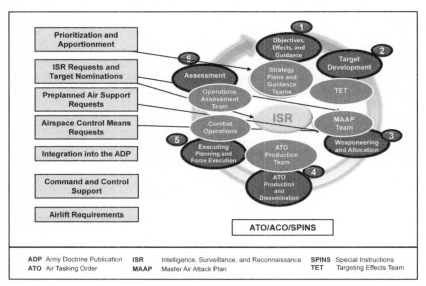

Figure 2-1. Event/time-driven events in the joint air tasking cycle.

17

> **Note:** It is important for the BCD plans section to understand the priorities of the ARFOR/Land Component Commander (LCC) and to read and understand the air operations directive (AOD) and the joint air operations plan (JAOP). By doing this, the plans team will better understand the ARFOR/ACC's 24-to-96 hour focus (input provided by intelligence plans officer).

In Figure 2-1, Command Post of the Future (CPOF) is not compatible with the Theater Battle Management Core System (TBMCS) and cannot be shared through the Immediate Response Information System (IRIS). The COP is also shared using other tools, such as Combined Information Data Network Exchange (CIDNE).

PERSONNEL

The BCD plans section consists of seven personnel: plans officer, deputy plans officer, targeting officer, senior fire support noncommissioned officer (NCO), targeting NCO, and two fire support sergeants. Duties and responsibilities are outlined below.

Plans Officer. The plans officer is the senior Army representative to the joint air operations center (JAOC) combat plans division, and is responsible for the overall functioning of the plans section of the BCD. His primary duty is coordinating with the JAOC staff to ensure the integration and synchronization of air and ARFOR operations. His duties also include providing information to ARFOR planners on the Joint Force Air Component Commander (JFACC) capabilities and plans. He informs the JAOC combat plans division of planned friendly operations, in addition to the scheme of maneuver, targeting concept and priorities, planned fire support coordination measures, munitions, or targeting restrictions that may affect air operations planning, air interdiction, and preplanned close air support requests. The plans officer also attends strategy division working group meetings as required, and keeps the BCD Commander informed of significant plans, issues, and problems pertaining to strategy and plans. He ensures the plans section has Joint Automated Deep Operations Coordination System (JADOCS), Advanced Field Artillery Tactical Data System (AFATDS), and Global Command and Control System-Army (GCCS-A) Windows NT workstations, which allow for effective cross talk about target management conduction within the operations, intelligence, and airlift sections.

Deputy Plans Officer. The deputy plans officer assists the plans officer and, when required, can perform as the plans officer. He receives, coordinates, and integrates the ARFOR air support requests (ASRs) into the air tasking order (ATO) development process; validates Army forces ASR priorities based upon intent and guidance of the Joint Force Commander (JFC) and the Commander, Army forces (COMARFOR); validates the timing of attack, and the desired effects; monitors the status and operation of ARFOR deep operations assets; supervises the operation of the ARFOR staff; and maintains information exchange with the ARFOR staff.

Targeting Officer. Targeting officer duties include supervising the preparation of target lists for targeting board meetings; validating the target list input from the Army forces; briefing target selection and justification; briefing ARFOR plans to the JAOC staff; and training personnel in the targeting and ATO development process. These duties are similar to those of a targeting officer at an ARFOR deep operations coordination cell (DOCC), fires and effects coordination cell (FECC), or fire support element (FSE).

Senior Fire Support NCO. The senior fire support NCO performs the duties of the section noncommissioned officer in charge (NCOIC), and is responsible for the overall setup and operation of the plans section. This includes supervising day-to-day section operations, operations of the section's Army Battle Command System (ABCS) equipment, and coordinating all the fire support coordination measures (FSCMs) with the joint expeditionary team (JET)/master air attack plan (MAAP) of the combat plans division.

Targeting NCO. In the absence of the targeting officer, the targeting NCO is responsible for performing the targeting officer duties. The targeting NCO is also in charge of map board maintenance, or depicting planned friendly situations on the map board or through command, control, communications, computers, and intelligence (C4I) systems; establishing and maintaining communications links with the ARFOR assistant chief of staff, operations (G3) plans section, the DOCC, and the FECC; and processing Army forces ASRs for air interdiction (AI) and close air support (CAS). The targeting NCO also assists the senior fire support NCO in the coordination and execution of day-to-day operations of the section.

Fire Support Sergeants. Fire support sergeants are the primary common operational picture (COP) workstation (JADOCS, AFATDS, and GCCS-A) operators. They are responsible for the setup and overall operation of the COP workstations. Duties include configuring and establishing communications, loading master unit data provided by ARFOR, ensuring the required digital maps are available, and performing operator preventive maintenance checks and services (PMCS) on the system and auxiliary equipment. They must also perform all other tasks as directed by the senior fire support NCO (e.g., the 19th BCD tactical operation).

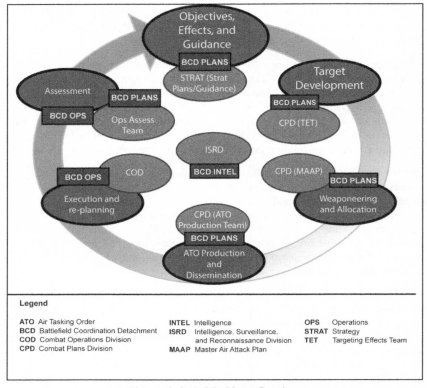

Figure 2-2. BCD Plans Section.

STRATEGY DIVISION/COMBAT PLANS DIVISION (KOREA-SPECIFIC EXAMPLE FROM 3RD BCD)

The plans section further organizes itself into three parts: strategy, targeting effects team (TET), and MAAP, with major efforts from 96 to 12 hours prior to execution of each air tasking order. The ATO is passed to the operations section upon publication, and the "plan" becomes real-time operations.

Strategy (96 to 72 Hours from ATO execution)

The plans officer in charge will work with the AOC strategy team in order to ensure the ARFOR/Joint Force Land Component Commander's (JFLCC's) intent and objectives are met during the development of the air operations directive. There are two distinct venues within the strategy section that enable this. The first venue is providing the AOC's strategy division with the Geographic Combatant Commander's (GCC's) intent, objectives, and scheme of maneuver for 96 hours out. Using this information, the BCD's strategy team advocates for the ARFOR/JFLCC during the production of the AOD. This is reflected in the AOD via the tactical tasks and tactical objectives. The second venue the strategy team can use to enable AOD development is input into the operational assessment. The strategy team represents the GCC's assessment of the "fight" and ensures that future apportionment and weights of effort support the GCC's plan.

Inputs to Strategy:

- Combined Forces Command, Korea (CFC) guidance

- The GCC's intent, operational objectives, and scheme of maneuver

- Operational orders

Outputs from Strategy:

- Air operations directive (AOD)

- Prioritized objectives in support of the CFC plan

- Weights of effort (low, medium, and high) and apportionment

- Operational and tactical objectives

Targeting Effects Team (72 to 48 Hours from ATO)

The targeting effects team utilizes the AOD and advocates for the ARFOR/ JFLCC's nominated targets to be added to the joint integrated prioritized target list (JIPTL), which is the CFC's prioritized list of targets and effects identified for action during a particular ATO period. The JIPTL draft is approved during the joint targeting coordination board (JTCB), which is chaired by the combined joint staff, operations (CJ3). The approved JIPTL is the primary output of the combined joint targeting coordination board (CJTCB), and the TET process. From there, the JTCB is handed off to the MAAP team, which then matches approved targets against available resources.

Inputs to TET:

- AOD

- Component target nominations

Outputs from TET:

- JIPTL

- Recommendations for modification of apportionment and weights of effort

Master Air Attack Plan Team (48 to 12 Hours from ATO Execution)

The JIPTL is sent to the BCD MAAP team for data entry into the Theater Battle Management Core System (TBMCS). The MAAP process begins with the MAAP changeover brief. The BCD MAAP team briefs the ARFOR/JFLCC's friendly and enemy ground situation to ensure the ARFOR/JFLCC's operations are integrated with the ACC's operations. After the MAAP changeover brief, the BCD MAAP team segregates the ARFOR/JFLCC's targets (on the approved JIPTL) by X-attack/air interdiction, and uploads them into the appropriate TBMCS system (the MAAP toolkit or theater air planner). Concurrently, pre-planned CAS requests arrive via secure means to the MAAP cell and are entered into TBMCS. Once the BCD MAAP cell uploads to the appropriate TBMCS system, the AOC MAAP team begins to pair these targets to available resources (aircraft, weapons, etc.). Once developed, the MAAP is pushed to the AOC's ATO production team in order to build the ATO. The ATO production team will publish the ATO no later than 12 hours prior to execution. At publication, the plans section will conduct a changeover brief of the ATO to the operations section on the floor for execution.

Inputs to the MAAP Cell:

- JIPTL

- Pre-planned CAS requests 1972 and D670

Outputs from the MAAP:

- Air Tasking Order/Special Instructions

- Airspace Control Order (3rd BCD tactical operation [TACOP])

ARMY INPUTS TO THE AIRSPACE CONTROL PLAN (ACP)

The ACP is written by the airspace control authority (ACA) and approved by the JFC. The ACP provides specific planning guidance and procedures for the airspace control system throughout the joint operation area (JOA). The ACP also establishes the airspace control system, procedures, and control nodes. The ACP may be distributed as an annex to the operations plan, or as a separate document.

As members of the airspace team in the air operations center, it is important for the BCD airspace management personnel to be engaged with the ACA's airspace managers during the ACP development process to ensure the Army's contribution to the airspace control system (ACS) is incorporated into the ACP. Some information one would expect to see in the Army's contribution would be: the Army organizations deployed to provide airspace control within the ground commander's area of operations (AO) (e.g., Air Defense Airspace Management [ADAM]/Brigade Aviation Management [BAE]), clearance of fires procedures (e.g., Army Tactical Missile System [ATACMS] and Guided Multiple Launch Rocket System [GMLRS]), and airspace control procedures (e.g., mission requirements request [MRR] nominations and airspace coordinating measure [ACM] naming conventions).

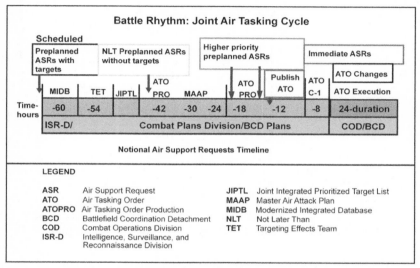

Figure 2-3. Battle Rhythm: Joint Air Tasking Cycle.

PROCESSING UNIT AIRSPACE PLANS (UAP)

By definition, the processing UAPs contain all the airspace plans a particular unit will need to perform its mission for any given ATO day. During planning, airspace element personnel at all echelons develop ACMs to support planned operations. These personnel use airspace control means requests (ACMREQs) to coordinate and integrate planned ACMs into higher headquarters as part of a future ACO.

Requests are consolidated at each echelon; ACMREQs form the basis of a unit's UAP. The U.S. message text format (USMTF) for the request form is 658 ACMREQ. As these UAPs are sent up the chain of command via the Tactical Airspace Integration System (TAIS), each higher echelon coordinates, consolidates, and integrates the plans until a single Army UAP exists at the ARFOR-level. Airspace element personnel send this ARFOR level UAP, which contains all the Army airspace requirements, to the BCD airspace management section for coordination with the ACA's airspace management team and inclusion into the appropriate ACO.[2]

23

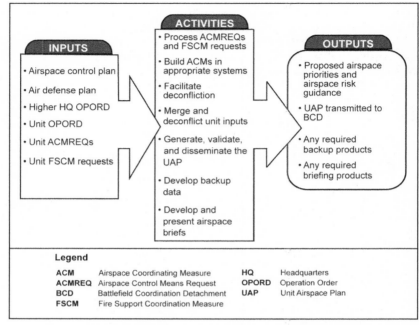

Figure 2-4. Development process for the unit airspace plan.

Endnotes

1. Army Techniques Publication (ATP) 3-09.13, *The Battlefield Coordination Detachment*, 24 JUL 2015.

2. Air Force Tactics, Techniques, and Procedures (AFTTP) 3-3.AOC, *Operational Employment-Air and Space Operations Center*, 17 MAR 2010.

CHAPTER 3

Training

HOME STATION TRAINING

Outside of formal schooling, the battlefield coordination detachment (BCD) conducts unit-level training on a variety of topics pertinent to its duty as the liaison between the theater Joint Force Land Component Commander (JFLCC) (and the designated Army forces (ARFOR) Commander) and the theater Joint Force Air Component Commander (JFACC). Professional development leadership classes cover subjects such as Pacific-theater-related operational plans (OPLANs), the joint targeting cycle, and the joint air targeting cycle. The BCD also provides an academic style brief entitled, "BCD Overview," to a variety of senior leaders across the Pacific.

Battle Drills

Below are battle drills that are codified in the tactical standard operating procedures (TACSOP).

Immediate: There are two battle drills associated with an immediate Army Tactical Missile System (ATACMS)/Guided Multiple Launch Rocket System (GMLRS)/Excalibur mission: (1) The JFACC may request the ARFOR ATACMS to attack a target, or (2) The ARFOR may attack a target by sending an ATACMS/GMLRS/Excalibur through JFACC airspace.

(1) Army Forces ATACMS/GMLRS/Excalibur mission: The ARFOR requests come to the operations section Advanced Field Artillery Tactical Data System (AFATDS) from the highest echelon fires cell. ATACMS fire missions are often time sensitive missions and need to be fired as soon as possible, so expedited airspace clearance is a prime concern. ATACMS fire missions should:

- Receive the ATACMS/GMLRS/Excalibur mission via AFATDS.

- Verify that the platoon area hazard, target area hazard, and missile flight path are passed to the BCD Airspace Management Section Tactical Airspace Integration System (TAIS).

- Track the fire mission via the BCD airspace management section and the Air Force (AF) airspace management team.

- Send clearance of fires upon approval from the AF airspace management team and the BCD airspace management section.

- Monitor the ATACMS/GMLRS/Excalibur mission and report end of mission to BCD airspace management section to reopen airspace for aircraft.

(2) JFACC ATACMS/GMLRS/Excalibur mission: The JFACC requests
follow a similar path as the Army forces' ATACMS requests, except the
5th BCD creates the target and sends it to the ARFOR fire cell for mission
processing. Once the ARFOR assigns firing units, the request will come
back through the operations section for airspace clearance using the
"ARFOR ATACMS/GMLRS/Excalibur mission" above.

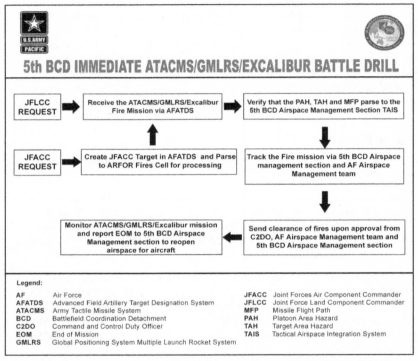

**Figure 3-1. Example of 5th BCD immediate ATACMS/GMLRS/
Excalibur battle drills.**

Immediate Air Support Request (ASR): Immediate air support missions
are only used when a request arises during the course of that air tasking
order (ATO) day. Immediate missions are those that cannot be identified far
enough in advance to permit detailed coordination and planning. Failure
to plan properly and get a timely air support request on the ATO day does
not constitute an immediate request. Often, immediate ASRs come at
the expense of preplanned missions. It is imperative that the operations
section understands the ARFOR guidance, intent, and priorities if it is
unable to confirm with the fires cell. When working an immediate request

quickly, the operations section should gather pertinent information and pass that information to the correct duty officer in close air support (CAS), intelligence, electronic warfare, or senior intelligence (Air Force). Then the operations section should work with the duty officer to coordinate the ASR quickly, as response time is the prime consideration. Prior to coordination, the operations section should ensure that the ARFOR has exhausted all means to support the request using allocated excess air support. These requests should come directly from the air support operations center (ASOC)/air support operation squadron (ASOS) to the duty officer, but can often come directly from the ARFOR. The different types of missions are:

(1) Immediate non-digital ASRs, which have many different mission types. The mission type determines how the mission is processed, and who the operations section must coordinate with in order to successfully support the mission.

- **Close Air Support (CAS).** Air action by fixed or rotary wing aircraft against hostile targets that are in close proximity to friendly forces (the distance in which some form of terminal attack control is required to prevent fratricide), and require detailed integration of each air mission (the level of coordination required to achieve desired effects while minimizing the risk of fratricide) with the fire and movement of those forces.[1]

    ○ **Air Alert-Close Air Support (X-CAS).** CAS in which the aircraft is airborne and available for a mission.

    ○ **Ground Alert-Close Air Support (G-CAS).** CAS in which the aircrew is standing by and can be airborne within ATO designated time.

- **Air Interdiction.** Interdiction operations are actions to divert, disrupt, delay, or destroy an enemy's surface capabilities before they can be used effectively against friendly forces or to otherwise achieve objectives. Interdiction operations may support the theater/joint operations area (JOA)-wide priorities or component operations.[2]

    ○ **Air Alert-Interdiction (X-INT).** Interdiction in which the aircraft is airborne and available for a mission.

    ○ **Ground Alert-Interdiction (G-INT).** Interdiction in which the aircrew is standing by and can be airborne within ATO designated time.

- **Intelligence, Surveillance, and Reconnaissance (ISR).** An activity that synchronizes and integrates the planning and operation of sensors, assets and processing, exploitation, and dissemination systems in direct support of current and future operations.[3]

27

- **Electronic Warfare (EW).** Any action involving the use of electromagnetic (EM) or directed energy (DE) to control the electromagnetic spectrum (EMS), or to attack the enemy. If the BCD is not augmented by an Army EW representative, direct communication with the fires cell EW representative is vital. Often, direct communication from the Army EW duty officer (EWDO) to the air operations center (AOC) EW officer director of operations is required.[4]

  - ○ **Electronic Attack (EA).** The subdivision of EW involving the use of EM energy, DE, or anti-radiation weapons to attack personnel, facilities, or equipment with the intent of degrading, neutralizing, or destroying enemy combat capability. It is considered a form of fires.

  - ○ **Electronic Protection (EP).**The subdivision of EW involving actions taken to protect personnel, facilities, and equipment from any effects of friendly or enemy use of the EMS that might degrade, neutralize, or destroy friendly combat capability.

  - ○ **Electronic Warfare Support (ES).**The subdivision of EW involving actions tasked by, or under direct control of, an operational commander to search for, intercept, identify, and locate or localize sources of intentional and unintentional radiated EM energy for the purpose of immediate threat recognition, targeting, planning, and conduct of future operations. (Source: The 5th BCD TACSOP, CARD 503)

(2) Digital procedures for immediate ASR when there is no air support operations center (ASOC).

- Receive immediate ASR via the Advanced Field Artillery Tactical Data System (AFATDS). DD Form 1972 Joint Tactical Air Strike Request, is used to request preplanned and immediate air support.

- Send immediate ASR into Web Air Request Processer (WARP) via AFATDS. Ensure the duty officer is tracking the immediate mission in WARP. Duty officers are often busy working multiple missions and tracking flights, so asking for the requested information (latitude/ longitude, etc.) from the target duty officer manually, or through the directed chat protocols, is usually the best course of action.

- Pass known information to the ARFOR (mission number, aircraft type, number of aircraft, call sign of aircraft, expected time on station) via AFATDS and/or telephone.

- Track the new mission via equipment status report until the mission is complete.

JOINT TACTICAL AIR STRIKE REQUEST	See Joint Pub 3-09.3 for preparation instructions.

SECTION I - MISSION REQUEST

1. UNIT CALLED	THIS IS	REQUEST NUMBER	DATE	
				SENT
			TIME	BY

2. PREPLANNED: [A] PRECEDENCE_____ [B] PRIORITY_____

   IMMEDIATE: [C] PRIORITY_____

	RECEIVED
TIME	BY

3. TARGET IS/NUMBER OF

[A] PERS IN OPEN_____ [B] PERS DUG IN_____ [C] WPNS/MG/RR/AT_____ [D] MORTARS, ARTY_____
[E] AAA ADA_____ [F] RKTS MISSILE_____ [G] ARMOR_____ [H] VEHICLES_____
[I] BLDGS_____ [J] BRIDGES_____ [K] PILLBOX, BUNKERS_____ [L] SUPPLIES, EQUIP_____
[M] CENTER (CP, COM)_____ [N] AREA_____ [O] ROUTE_____ [P] MOVING N E S W_____
[O] REMARKS

4. TARGET LOCATION IS

[A]_____ [B]_____ [C]_____ [D]_____ BY

(COORDINATES) (COORDINATES) (COORDINATES) (COORDINATES)

[E] TGT ELEV_____ [F] SHEET NO._____ [G] SERIES_____ [H] CHART NO._____

CHECKED

5. TARGET TIME/DATE

[A] ASAP_____ [B] NLT_____ [C] AT_____ [D] TO_____

6. DESIRED ORD/RESULTS [A] ORDNANCE_____

[B] DESTROY_____ [C] NEUTRALIZE_____ [D] HARASS/INTERDICT_____

7. FINAL CONTROL

[A] FAC/RABFAC_____ [B] CALL SIGN_____ [C] FREQ_____

[D] CONT PT_____

8. REMARKS

1. IP_____

2. HDNG_____ MAG_____ OFFSET: L/R_____

3. DISTANCE_____

4. TGT ELEVATION_____ FEET MSL

5. TGT DESCRIPTION_____

6. TGT LOCATION_____

7. MARK TYPE_____ CODE_____

8. FRIENDLIES_____

9. EGRESS_____

THE FOLLOWING MAY BE INCLUDED IN THE "REMARKS", IF REQUIRED:

BCN-TGT_____ MAG_____ BCN GRID_____ /_____

BCN-TGT_____ METERS_____ TGT GRID_____ /_____

BCN ELEVATION_____ FEET MSL

SECTION II - COORDINATION

9. NSFS	10. ARTY	11. AIO/G-2/G-3

12. REQUEST	13. BY	14. REASON FOR DISAPPROVAL
☐ APPROVED ☐ DISAPPROVED		

15. RESTRICTIVE FIRE/AIR PLAN
[A] IS NOT IN EFFECT [B] NUMBER_____

16. IS IN EFFECT
[A] (FROM TIME)_____ [B] (TO TIME)_____

17. LOCATION
[A]_____ [B]_____
(FROM COORDINATES) (TO COORDINATES)

18. WIDTH (METERS)_____

19. ALTITUDE/VERTEX
[A]_____ [B]_____
(MAXIMUM/VERTEX) (MINIMUM)

SECTION III - MISSION DATA

20. MISSION NUMBER	21. CALL SIGN	22. NO. AND TYPE AIRCRAFT	23. ORDNANCE
24. EST/ACT TAKEOFF	25. EST TOT	26. CONT PT (COORDS)	27. INITIAL CONTACT
28. FAC/FAC(A)/TAC(A) CALL SIGN/ FREQ	29. AIRSPACE COORDINATION AREA	30. TGT DESCRIPTION	*31. TGT COORD/ELEV

32. BATTLE DAMAGE ASSESSMENT (BDA) REPORT (USMTF INFLTREP)

LINE 1/CALL SIGN_____   LINE 4/LOCATION_____

LINE 2/MSN NUMBER_____   LINE 5/TOT_____

LINE 3/REQ NUMBER_____   LINE 6/RESULTS_____

REMARKS_____   *TRANSMIT AS APPROPRIATE

DD FORM 1972, APR 2003	PREVIOUS EDITION MAY BE USED.	[Reset]	Adobe Professional 7.0

Figure 3-2. DD Form 1792.

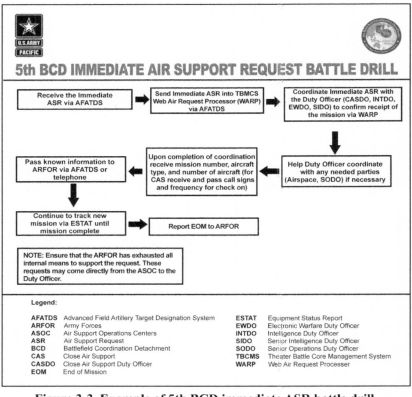

Figure 3-3. Example of 5th BCD immediate ASR battle drill.

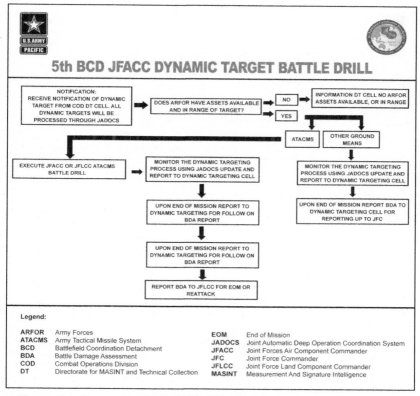

Figure 3-4. Example of 5th BCD JFACC dynamic target battle drill.

Dynamic Targeting: Monitor and manage the dynamic targeting process using the Joint Automated Deep Operations Coordination System (JADOCS) manager, directed by the combat operations division (COD). When requested by the dynamic targeting cell, clear time-sensitive targets (TSTs)/high-payoff targets (HPTs) with the ARFOR for attack, and then process the BCD field in the appointed target manager accordingly (i.e., the dynamic target manager or the AOC target manager).

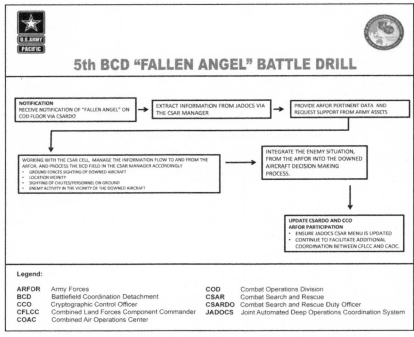

Figure 3-5. 5th BCD Fallen Angel battle drill.

DEPARTMENT OF THE ARMY
4ᵗʰ BATTLEFIELD COORDINATION DETACHMENT
850 DRYDEN WAY BUILDING 1923
SHAW AIR FORCE BASE, SOUTH CAROLINA 29152

ACBC-CO   20 February 2019

MEMORANDUM FOR RECORD

SUBJECT: Training Certification for (Rank/Name): _____

1. I certify that the above named Soldier has completed the following training requirements within the specified time frames below. I have initialed either <u>YES</u> or <u>NO</u> for each requirement.

REQUIREMENTS	Supervisor INITIALS		DATE COMPLETED
	YES	NO	
Anti-Terrorism Level 1 – **(annually)**			
ISOPREP On File in PRMS **(Update within D-90)**			
Operational Security (OPSEC) **(annually)**			
Combating Trafficking in Persons **(annually)**			
Report Intelligence Information **(annually)**			
Cultural Awareness (Country Designation Brief) **(annually)**			
SERE 100.2 Code of Conduct Training Course **(Valid for 3 years)**			
USCENTCOM Moderate/High Risk of Isolation Theater Brief (MRI/HRI) **(Valid for 2 years)**			
TBI Awareness/Army Concussion Course **(annually)**			
350-1 Training Requirements **(see App 5 to Annex B)**			

2. POC for this memorandum is (Section OIC)_____.

Andrew Shaffer   GEOFFREY R. ADAMS
MAJ, FA   COL, AD
Operations   Commanding

Figure 3-6. Memo for 4th BCD training certification.

COMBAT TRAINING CENTER (CTC) ROTATIONS

Green Flag-West (GFW) is the Air Force's premier flag exercise; it directly supports the Army's National Training Center (NTC) rotations. GFW is one of the only joint Army and AF exercises that can facilitate joint fires integration at the brigade (BDE) level against a near-peer adversary in a challenging and contested tactical environment. Currently, the AF uses GFW as a validation exercise for each fighter/bomber squadron prior to their deployment.

Much like the critter teams at the NTC (Wolf, Bronco, Raven, etc.), the 549th Combat Training Squadron, based out of Nellis Air Force Base (AFB), Nevada, is charged with providing advanced, realistic, and relevant air-to-surface training that allows joint and coalition warfighters to meet the Combatant Commander's requirements across air, space, and cyberspace.

The 379th Ground Liaison Detachment (GLD), which belongs to the 5th BCD, is attached to the 549th Combat Training School (CTS). The 379th GLD provides white force support, support observer-controller/trainers (OC/Ts) to rotational GLOs, and Army academics to each GFW rotation. The GLO is an integral part of the CAS kill team. It is at this venue that the GLO provides a brief, in conjunction with AF intelligence, that gives the pilots a common operational picture of the BDE battlespace. The GLO gives the most up-to-date friendly and enemy forces situation, to include scheme of maneuver, artillery positions, the Ground Commander's intent for CAS, and preplanned/immediate air tasking (DD Form 1972). This update provides shared understanding among AF pilots and the Army remote thermal unit (RTU), which sets the conditions for rapid and smooth persecution of enemy targets in the BDE's battlespace.

EXERCISES

The 5th BCD conducts multiple training exercises over the course of a year, to include Fleet Synthetic Training, Ulchi Freedom Guardian, Yama Sakura, Talisman Saber, Pacific Sentry, Cobra Gold, Rim of the Pacific, Key Resolve, and Orient Shield. Yama Sakura, Talisman Saber, and Pacific Sentry provide opportunities for the BCD to train on all BCD mission-essential task list (METL) tasks, including:

- 06-DET-2109, Process a JFACC request for Army Forces Assets

- 06-DET-2128, Prepare Information System Platforms and Collaborative Tools for Operation

- 06-DET-5126, Coordinate ARFOR Fires Beyond the Fire Support Coordination Line (FSCL)

- 06-DET-5133, Integrate ARFOR/Land Component Requirements During the Joint Air Tasking Cycle.

These exercises specifically allow the 5th BCD to train on all Objective-T METL tasks in a dynamic and complex environment.

Yama Sakura is a Tier 1 exercise, offering opportunities to enhance relationships with both joint and bilateral partners while establishing and practicing tactics, techniques, and procedures (TTPs).

Talisman Saber demonstrates operational readiness as a combined BCD (C-BCD) to integrate joint air support in unified land operations (ULOs). It enables agile mission command at the component level in preparation for potential combined and joint operations in the Indo-Pacific area of responsibility. For the 5th BCD specifically, Talisman Saber includes the Australian 16th Air Land Regiment. During Talisman Saber, the 5th BCD demonstrated their operational readiness as a C-BCD to integrate joint air support in ULOs. As mentioned previously, agile mission command is at the component-level, in preparation for potential combined and joint operations in the Pacific. The 5th BCD combined with the Australian BCD, have improved interoperability and increased the Australian joint air land integration cell (JALIC) capacity for air-ground integration.]

Primary training audiences for Pacific Sentry are the U.S. Army, Pacific Command (USARPAC), the Theater Joint Force Land Component Commander (TJFLCC), 8th Army, and the United States Forces, Korea (USFK). Its secondary training audience is the 8th Theater Support Command (TSC), the 94th Army Air and Missile Defense Command (AAMDC), the 5th BCD, 311th Signal (SIG) Command, and the 500th Military Intelligence (MI) Brigade. Pacific Sentry operationalizes U.S. Indo-Pacific Command (USINDOPACOM) headquarters (HQ) and allows for the periodic review and refinement of critical plans; evaluates theater logistical/operational sustainment capability, and ensures theater Army support is ready and available. This provides the opportunity for the BCD airlift section to train on its METL subtask 06-DET-5114, Coordinate for Validated Strategic/Tactical Airlift/Airdrop Requests.

As the higher echelon and supervising operational headquarters for ground liaison detachments (GLDs), the BCD is responsible for the formal training/readiness of GLD assigned personnel.

TRAINING

All BCD personnel must be qualified in their military occupational specialty (MOS) as early in their assignment as possible. When qualified, BCD personnel can focus on collective and follow-on training, in addition to the sustainment of individual skills. Duties in the BCD are highly technical in nature. Much of the individual training comes from the wide variety of courses taught at the various Service schools. The BCD conducts section collective training and joint training exercises.

FORMAL TRAINING

Under ideal conditions, all members of the BCD should attend formal (i.e., schoolhouse) training. Currently, BCD personnel require a priority to attend courses most related to their MOS. BCD personnel also need to attend courses that are not directly related to their MOS, in order to give the BCD a cross-trained capability. Cross training enhances the BCD's flexibility, allowing it to tailor support for contingencies when a full BCD has not been deployed.

BCD personnel should attend the following courses as appropriate for their duty position:

• Joint Air Operations Command and Control Course

• Joint Aerospace Operations Senior Staff Course

• Air Operations Center Initial Qualifications Course

• Joint Targeting Staff Course

• Joint Targeting Applications Course

The BCD-recommended training tables can be found in Army Techniques Publication (ATP) 3-09.12, *The Battlefield Coordination Detachment*, 24 JUL 2015.

Operations with the U.S. Navy (USN) or U.S. Marine Corps (USMC) could be either land-or-sea based; BCD members selected to conduct operations with the USN or USMC should receive the following training:

• Training in the terms and shipboard procedures specific to the USN and USMC.

• Water and survival frequent flyer training, no later than 30 days prior to scheduled training with the USN or USMC. (Required training prior to deployment.)

• Supporting Arms Coordination Center Course at the Naval Amphibious Base, Little Creek, Virginia. The Supporting Arms Coordination Center Course orients personnel on the functioning of the Supporting Arms Coordination Center and Tactical Air Coordination Center afloat, and includes a walkthrough of shipboard facilities in the Naval shipyard. Shipboard communications are extensively addressed.

• Amphibious Indoctrination Course at Naval Amphibious Base, Little Creek, Virginia.

• USMC Air Weapons Tactical Squadron Course at Marine Corps Air Station Yuma, Arizona.

The following list details United States Central Command (USCENTCOM) specific courses and 4th BCD training methodology:

- Military occupational specialty (MOS)/position-specific 505th Command and Control Wing courses. The primary course is the Air and Space Operations Center-Individual Qualification Training. The Joint Air and Space Operations Command and Control course is an accepted substitute.

- Attendance at a division warfighter exercise (typically executed at Hurlburt Field, Florida).

- BCD internal training on the Army Battle Command System (ABCS)/ Mission Command Systems; area of responsibility (AOR) familiarity with routine situation reports (SITREPs) from forward campaign headquarters; and weekly operations and intelligence briefings. See Figure 3-6 for an example of internal training certification for deploying servicemembers in addition to theater-specific training requirements.

Note: Ground liaison officers (GLOs) utilize a similar methodology but usually attend Green Flag-West (supporting either their squadron or one they will deploy with) as opposed to a division warfighter exercise. GLOs will also attend the Joint Fires and Effects Course at Nellis Air Force Base, Nevada.

European-theater-specific courses available:

- Joint Combat Operations Course at the U.S. Air Forces in Europe Air-Ground Operations School, Sembach Kaserne, Germany. This course focuses on the integration of U.S. Armed Forces into the North Atlantic Treaty Organization (NATO) area of responsibility.

- NATO Air Ground Operations at Dorset, United Kingdom. This course provides instruction in the principles, planning, and conduct of joint conventional offensive and defensive air operations in the multinational command of Europe NATO battle group.

The continuous upgrading of automation hardware and software creates the need for constant operator training on automated systems currently fielded to the BCD. This training includes, but is not limited to:

- Global Combat Support System-Army (GCCS-A) operator training at home station, and interface training during joint exercises, to include proficiency enhancement in the Army Mission Command System (AMCS) and the Theater Battle Management Core System (TBMCS) applications, tools, and interfaces.

- Advanced Field Artillery Tactical Data System (U.S. Army) operator and supervisor training, provided at the U.S. Army Fires Center of Excellence.

- Tactical Airspace Integration System (TAIS) digital master gunner training, taught at the U.S. Army Aviation Center of Excellence (USAACE). This course provides the formal TAIS operator training required for this position.

- The air and missile defense workstation training, also provided at the USAACE.

- Selected BCD personnel should receive training in the Airborne Warning and Control System and/or Joint Surveillance and Target Attack Radar System operations, and be prepared to deploy early during contingency operations as an Army liaison from the BCD until theater communications and mission command capabilities mature.

Korea-theater-specific courses available are:

- Army Space Cadre Basic Course

- Advanced Field Artillery Tactical Data System

- Chemical, Biological, Radiological, Nuclear, and Explosive (CBRNE) School

- Command Post of the Future Advance (CPOF Advance)

- Joint Automated Deep Operations Coordination System

- Joint Capabilities Release

- Total Ammunition Management Information System

- Joint Operational Fires and Effects Course

TRAINING TASK LIST

Training objectives for individual training should focus on the following mission task list:

- Know basic joint doctrine for each of the Services, including missions and organizations for combat.

- Comprehend the command, control, communications, computers, and intelligence systems; related procedures; and coordination associated with air and surface support to joint operations.

- Apply intelligence and other information from all sources to the decision-making process for joint operations.

• Know threat systems and the doctrinal force employment concepts U.S. forces will likely encounter in the proposed theater of operations.

• Know missions and major weapons systems used by U.S. forces in joint operations.

• Know concepts, capabilities, limitations, and operational procedures for combat targeting; the joint suppression of enemy air defenses; cyber electromagnetic activities; reconnaissance; airlift; special operations; and space support to joint operations.

• Understand the Army's military decisionmaking process for planning, coordination, control, and execution of integrated joint operations at the operational level of war.

• Comprehend and apply knowledge of airspace control procedures and measures that support the ARFOR commander's activity in joint operations.

• Know the air battle plan and the air tasking order process, the joint force and Army inputs to the ATO cycle, and ATO products of the ATO cycle.

• Know the difference between the ATO and air battle plan.

• Know the contribution of the BCD to the development and execution of the air battle plan, ATOs, and airspace control orders (ACOs).

• When required, use the Theater Battle Management Core System tools to extract the air battle plan data. Understand higher-level TBMCS applications support to joint operations.

• Know the U.S. message text format system.

• Know the value of using web-based applications to view data in the air battle plan.

ENVIRONMENTAL PROTECTION

Protection of natural resources has become an ever-increasing concern in Army training programs. All unit leaders have the responsibility to reduce and, if possible, eliminate damage to the environment when conducting training. Additionally, commanders must ensure that units and personnel are prepared to survive, defend, and continue operations in or near a contaminated area. Presence of critical facilities, such as nuclear power plants or chemical plants, could impact operations. Environmental risk management parallels safety risk management and is based on the same philosophy and principles. For further information, see ATP 5-19, *Risk Management*, 14 APR 2014.

Endnotes

1. Joint Publication (JP) 3-09.3, *Close Air Support*, 25 NOV 2014. CAC access required.

2. JP 3-03, *Joint Interdiction*, 09 SEPT 2016.

3. Ibid.

4. JP 3-13.1, *Electronic Warfare*, 08 FEB. 2012. CAC access required.

CHAPTER 4

Battlefield Coordination Detachment (BCD) Insights, Lessons, and Best Practices

TRAINING

Air Defense Artillery (ADA)

The Area Air Defense Commander (AADC) is normally the component commander with the best air defense capability, and the command, control, communications, and intelligence capability for planning and executing integrated air defense operations. The Joint Forces Air Component Commander (JFACC) may be designated as the joint force AADC. When the JFACC is also the AADC, the BCD eases coordination between Army forces (ARFOR) air and missile defense operations and the JFACC staff. The BCD helps the JFACC staff integrate JFACC defensive counter air operations with ground air defense systems. This BCD function is key to effective air defense and preventing fratricide.

The BCD may be the first ARFOR agency aware of the presence of a theater missile defense (TMD) target through sources at the joint air operations center (JAOC). In this case, the BCD uses the most efficient means available to help coordinate the rapid attack of TMD targets. With regard to TMD, the BCD does the following:

• Speeds target confirmation

• Deconflicts airspace

• Provides early warning to friendly ADA headquarters

The ADA section supports both the BCD plans and operations sections. The ADA section coordinates the Commander, Army forces (COMARFOR) air defense artillery matters with the JAOC combat plans and operations divisions and the ARFOR ADA headquarters. Digital information systems support the exchange and coordination of air defense and airspace management information. The ADA section coordinates with the ARFOR air defense element and the ADA brigade headquarters for the following:

• Locations of ADA assets

• Engagement reporting

• ADA weapon engagement zones

- Identification, friend or foe (IFF)/selective identification feature (SIF) procedures

- Receipt of ADA annexes to operation plans (OPLANs)/operation orders (OPORDs)

- Advising the AADC on Army air defense matters appropriate for the deconfliction of air support to ground operations

- Coordinating the following with the control and reporting center:

  o ADA unit status

  o Changes in air defense warning conditions

  o Weapons control status

  o Rules of engagement

  o Identification procedures

  o Early warning and theater ballistic missile (TBM) alert procedures

- Advising the senior air defense officer (SADO) in the JAOC of Army air defense status, to include:

  o Placement of ADA weapons in direct support of ground forces

  o Providing Army ADA commander with the AADC's intent

  o Coordinating with the ARFOR TMD cell for TBM alert dissemination procedures

  o Exchanging ADA operational data with JAOC counterparts

  o Coordinating ADA airspace needs with the JAOC airspace management and BCD airspace management sections

  o Supporting the integration of the COMARFOR area air defense plan with the JFACC counter air effort

Real World Operations[1]

The battlefield coordination detachment has been looking at the airspace challenge in Europe, but it is fairly complex and not entirely solvable by the U.S. unilaterally, though the U.S. Army arguably has the ability to significantly influence or fix elements of it. The problem, as understood currently, is across the doctrine, organization, training, materiel, leadership and education, personnel, facilities, and policy (DOTMLPF-P) spectrum, and the U.S. Army must outline what efforts it has taken, or is currently in the process of taking, in order to address or progress some of these issues. This includes the Army's efforts at dynamic force.

Doctrine

Generally, U.S. doctrine is sound, but will need to incorporate a tactical-level focus as airspace users become more common at the lower level. With the appearance of miniature unmanned aerial vehicles (UAVs) and swarm technology, the airspace below the coordinating altitude is becoming more and more congested. The larger problem doctrinally is on the North Atlantic Treaty Organization (NATO) side, which has been unable to come to a consensus on how to address the challenges of large-scale combat operations and their impact on airspace integration. This is largely attributed to the NATO Air Force community, who are working as the air coordination authorities and are unable to grasp the impact and scale of Army equities (mostly artillery equities) in the airspace equation. Much of the BCD's time is spent trying to help air command (AIRCOM) develop one of their already existing doctrinal geometries' high-density airspace control zones (HIDACZs), to be able to fulfill the functions that would be characterized as a coordinating altitude. Interestingly, AIRCOM has the HIDACZ within its doctrine, but does not specify the procedural application about who can control what enters the HIDACZ, or the standards that qualify a controlling/establishing agency to employ it. This is likely linked to the organizational shortfalls.

Organization

Manning shortfalls that are associated with the duties of the joint force land component commander (JFLCC) can significantly impede the ability of this airspace management function. Structurally, this extends to all levels (i.e., missing corps, missing division, partial combat aviation brigade). The proper development of the operation plan (OPLAN) cannot occur until these gaps are filled. It is unrealistic to put the weight of "Setting the Theater" from an airspace perspective on the shoulders of one or two planners at the Army Service component command (ASCC) level. The lower levels must exist to some degree in order to provide more detailed planning and substance to an unmanned aerial platform (UAP), and allow follow-on time-phased force and deployment data (TPFDD) units to have their initial bed-down locations and marching orders. This is fixable on the Army side.

On the NATO side, the application of U.S. doctrine in a European construct is problematic because there is a structural misalignment across the nations of the alliance. Several key allies and NATO force structures have examined, but not yet adopted, the joint air-ground integration center (JAGIC), and the legacy structures that are in place. These legacy structures are used to replicate the functionality of air support operations centers (ASOCs), most notably the air operations coordination centers (AOCCs). Bilateral air operation coordination centers are no longer equipped, trained, or expected to provide procedural control or extensive support to dynamic operations.

Training

Airspace managers coming into the European theater must be proficient in both U.S. and NATO systems of record. Integrated command and control (ICC) systems are not currently taught on the U.S. institutional side, but are taught at several courses conducted by NATO, most notably the initial functional joint force air component (JFAC) training. This is conducted at several locations including Kalkar, Germany, and Poggio Renatico, Italy. Further, U.S. airspace managers coming to theater should have a theater immersion course, which would familiarize them with NATO standards (specifically Supply Plan Mike — the AIRCOM standard operating procedures [SOP] governing airspace). This is critical in order to understand how terms of reference differ between U.S.-only operations, and those that are within Europe.

Materiel

Among airspace management systems of record, interoperability is a significant challenge, and goes beyond whether ICC can pass message traffic to the Tactical Airspace Integration System (TAIS). The short answer is "yes they can," but the interface is clunky as there is no direct technical linkage. This requires the operators to manually pull exported United States message text format (USMTF) files/formats for input into TAIS. This is accomplished by either passing disks, or by copy-paste out of chat windows (as demonstrated at Dynamic Front 2018, or DF18).

> **Note:** The ICC systems do not address, and are not currently an efficient platform for, enabling fires. The best example of this is that ICC cannot derive the missile flight path of an ATACMS the way TAIS can, and thus the BCD is relegated to the employment of "Hot Walls" or "Goal Posts."
>
> "Hot Walls" or "Goalposts" (Figures 4-1 and 4-2 respectively) are tactics, techniques, and procedures (TTP) to quickly block off airspace. A "Hot Wall" is one solid wall of airspace between the launch and target grids. However, this form of airspace coordinating measure (ACM) is not very flexible, as it blocks a large piece of airspace.
>
> A "Goalpost" is two funnels of airspace at the launch and target sites and a high-level corridor joining the two funnels. Goalposts allow for more flexible use of airspace, as they permit aircraft operations to continue between the funnels and below the corridor.

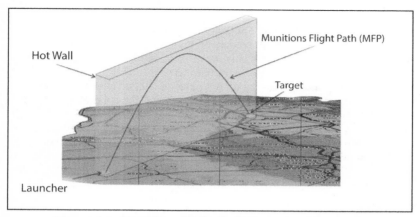

Figure 4-1. Munitions Flight Path Example (Hot Wall).

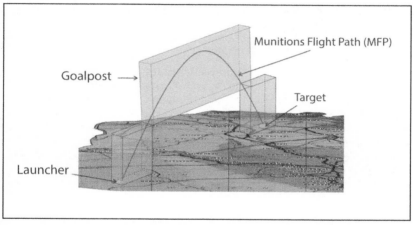

Figure 4-2. Munitions Flight Path Example (Goalpost).

Materially, the problems with the ICC system are fixable, cross-domain solutions notwithstanding. The larger issue is the lack of vertical integration of airspace systems along the alliance side. In rare instances on the NATO side, ICC extends down to the division level, but in most cases resides only at the corps level. Because airspace users are found more and more at lower levels (even the brigade level in terms of UAVs) there is an obvious disconnect, and the data that feeds the larger theater picture never makes it past the funnels of human interoperability at the data entry level. Furthermore, the functionality of ICC more closely resembles the Theater Battlefield Management Core System (TBMCS) than TAIS.

45

Leadership

In addition to requisite training at the user level, there needs to be continuous emphasis to senior leaders on the importance of airspace deconfliction and integration. Many allies, specifically the newer Eastern European allies, are disinclined to think in terms of the full scope joint air/land integration. Nations that do not have developed systems for the integration of airspace alongside of fire control and fire support systems are fundamentally still cognitively linked to the "Big Sky Little Bullet" theory. The "Big Sky Little Bullet" theory refers to the thought that rockets/missiles shot from the ground will not interrupt the airspace required for fixed-wing/rotary-wing aircraft because of the vast airspace available. This thought plays itself out in NATO exercises, which are not adequately detailed in the type of unit airspace plans required for operations.

Personnel

Aside from enduring theater personnel shortfalls, rotational units need to come prepared for the complexity of this non-familiar environment. Bottom line up front, a general support battalion combat aviation brigade (CAB) without an air traffic service company is problematic.

Facilities

As the Army collaborates with various air operations centers (AOCs) (i.e., NATO, multinational, and U.S.) in support of exercises or operations, it needs to understand the capabilities and limitations of those structures/organizations and what they provide. Many countries, such as those in the Baltics, do not have national AOCs, and rely on multilateral agreements to fulfill their needs. If the AOC the Army partners with is not the 603rd AOC, its level of technical interoperability will be diminished, and the recognized air picture degraded. This has to be a known risk during mission planning.

Policy

From a policy perspective, the challenges of airspace management in Europe are matters of strategic and operational significance. At no time should it be assumed that the U.S. will ever have unrestricted use of European air, even after the commencement of hostilities. Currently most, if not all, deviations from published flight plans require adaptations to diplomatic clearances. (This was lesson further identified during Saber Strike 18.) The U.S. needs to remain engaged and in close coordination with civil authorities (including, but not limited to, European control). As such, U.S. forces need to be realistic about their expectations of the Air Force as they, like the Army, are guests in European skies. The Air Force's degree of influence will be greater than the Army's, based on long-held relationships and regular engagements.

Figure 4-3 on the next page provides a summary of the airspace gap assessment.

Finally, as the 19th BCD assesses the problem, the U.S. Army is binning things into varying degrees of complexity:

1) Things U.S. Army Europe (USAREUR) can fix.

2) Things USAREUR, in coordination with Headquarters, Department of the Army (HQDA)/Big Army, can fix.

3) Things requiring joint collaboration.

4) Things requiring allied collaboration.

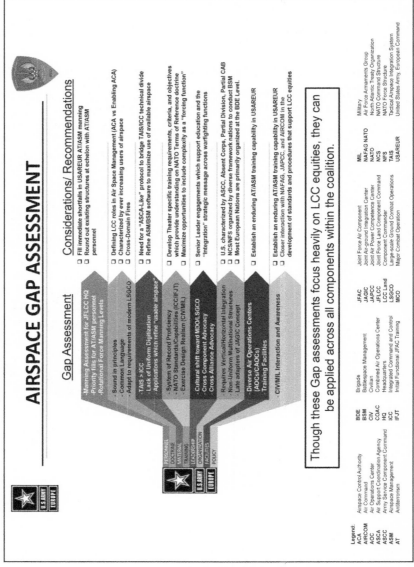

Figure 4-3. Airspace Gap Assessment.

Information Technology Team

The BCD's wartime mission is to deconflict both the ground and airspace on the battlefield. It is imperative that all Army Battle Command Systems (ABCSs) are operational and integrated within the JAOC. To meet this challenging mission, the system administrator (SYSAD) staff and the ABCS operators build interpersonal relationships with their respective counterparts. For SYSAD, the JAOC communication planner, or command, control, communication, computers and intelligence (C4I) tactical integrator, is the lead person responsible for assisting in this process, and leads and supervises the planning, resourcing, and execution of all information systems and network responsibilities for the BCD. The information technology (IT) team helps establish upper and lower tactical internet and all other communication equipment within the JAOC joint environment. Additionally, the SYSAD is the primary advisor to the detachment commander on matters as they relate to the employment of signal equipment and personnel. The team coordinates for support in any information management discipline. The IT team monitors and controls all automation requests and upgrades within the detachment. It oversees the execution of the detachment information management officer, the telephone control officer, the cryptographic control officer, and the training and awareness officer.

4th Battlefield Coordination Detachment

Based on the requirement for a continuous presence forward in the combined air operations center (CAOC), 4th BCD Soldiers maintain the following systems to ensure they can accomplish all associated missions:

Temporary change of station orders: Operations and plans personnel ensure that all deploying personnel have the required orders to go forward. This process requires management of dwelling considerations and an understanding of forward requirements, such as the specific clearances for specific positions.

Rotators and commercial flights: Similar to the orders process, the 4th BCD airlift section schedules and tracks flights for deploying personnel.

Ground liaison officer (GLO) support: The 4th BCD closely monitors United States Air Force (USAF) fighter/bomber positioning across the U.S. central command (CENTCOM) area of responsibility (AOR), to ensure that ground forces receive adequate support via ground liaisons. This requires frequent engagement with USAF central force management personnel. Additionally, the 4th BCD coordinates with the U.S. Navy Liaison Element (NALE) at the CAOC to provide GLO support to Carrier Air Wings that are conducting close air support (CAS) or dual capable aircraft missions in support of CENTCOM operations.

Note: All BCDs support squadrons that are deploying to the CENTCOM AOR with GLOs, as outlined in the 2011 Memorandum of Agreement.

CENTCOM CAOC specific manning considerations:

Battle cab: The COAC current operations position associated with the standard combat operations division (COD) floor is augmented with positions in the battle cab. The battle cab is a non-doctrinal operations center where the CAOC director (one-star general, or foreign equivalent), deputy CAOC director (U.S. colonel), and battle director (colonel, or foreign equivalent) can rapidly adapt to arising situations, or situations that require involvement from the Combined Forces Air Component Commander (CFACC) or D eputy CFACC. This position places BCD Soldiers, typically majors and senior noncommissioned officers (NCOs), with senior leaders where situational understanding and battle tracking are at a premium.

Airlift: Recently, the CFACC shifted the vast majority of the air mobility division back to the United States. The 4th BCD adjusted to this, and now maintains 24-hour operations at home station to fulfill this requirement.

GREEN FLAG-WEST NATIONAL TRAINING CENTER SUPPORT LESSONS LEARNED, AND TACTICS, TECHNIQUES, AND PROCEDURES

Lessons and Best Practices

A. National Training Center (NTC) Rotations

1. Issue: DD Form 1972 vetting and quality

Discussion: A brigade (BDE) is conducting a targeting cycle; however, the outputs (i.e., targeting packets) from the BDE targeting working group are not making it to the 1972s for the corresponding days. 1972s continue to be generic in nature.

Recommendation: The tactical air control party (TACP), specifically the air liaison officer (ALO), needs to be plugged into the targeting working group, and have complete oversight of the 1972 process. Once the Brigade Commander receives and approves the targeting nominations from the working group, the BDE fire support element (FSE) must place the targets allocated to close air support platforms into the 1972s with concrete targeting data (i.e., gridded reference graphics [GRGs], named areas of interest [NAIs], target areas of interest [TAIs], and graphics). This will reduce the amount of loiter time when CAS checks in on station.

2. Issue: Why are fixed-wing assets bringing the majority of their munitions back home?

Discussion: Currently, fixed-wing platforms are bringing a large amount of munitions back home. The primary reason identified in the joint after action report (JAAR) is the lack of a game plan for CAS as they check in on station. For example, the check-in of identified target sets, and the handoff between BDE plans and BDE current operations (CUOPS) at the check-in station. Additionally, it appears that the BDE S2 collection plan is disjointed. NAIs are not tied to an observer/collection method, which in turn cannot then confirm nor deny the commander's priority intelligence requirements.

Recommendation: The BDE needs to ensure the proper hand off between BDE plans and BDE CUOPS. More specifically, the BDE battle captain needs to understand the following:

  1) When CAS platforms are checking in.

  2) The brigade commander's daily intent for CAS.

  3) Understand what is on the 1972s (i.e., specific tasking versus shiny object syndrome).

If the handoff between plans and CUOPS is done correctly, it would mitigate some of the dynamic last minute re-tasking of aircraft, usually to non-traditional intelligence, surveillance, and reconnaissance (NTISR).

3. Issue: Updating their common operational picture (COP)

Discussion: The BDE and the TACP continued to reference graphics that were not on Command Post of the Future (CPOF). For example, the brigade created phase lines well into the operation, and did not push out an updated COP on CPOF, or on other means of communication. (i.e., transverse, military intelligence readiness command [MIRC], BDE liaison officers [LNOs].) This created confusion between the GLO and the pilots who then could not reference the graphics used by the TACP.

Recommendation: The COP at the brigade level needs to be on CPOF. BDE enablers, such as CAS, the Multi Launch Rocket System (MLRS), and other outside agencies, use CPOF as their primary means of establishing situational awareness. If the BDE COP is not on CPOF, it is the battle NCO's responsibility to ensure that CPOF is up to date.

4. Issue: Improving CAS integration at NTC from a ground LNO perspective

Discussion: The GLO and his ground liaison detachment (GLD) NCO serve as the primary coordinating element between the supported Air Force unit and the ground forces. Their key tasks are to provide detailed operational situational awareness (the COP, macro understanding of the overall battle space, etc.) to supported air crews; develop an understanding of various communications/digital capabilities (knowledge of Secret Internet Protocol Router Network [SIPRNET]/Non-Classified Internet Protocol Router Network [NIPRNET], CPOF, Joint Capabilities Release [JCR], chat platforms, Falcon View, Microsoft software, etc.); understand supported aircraft capabilities (targeting, simulated combat load, vulnerability times, general weaponeering and tactics, etc.); and understand the air tasking order process (DD Form 1972 flow from initiation to ATO publication, immediate and preplanned, etc.).

Recommendations:

> **Home station training with the TACP/ALO:** The TACP needs to train with the unit during the brigade combat team (BCT), battalion (BN), and BDE level validation exercises. If the TACP and ALO are meeting the BDE/BN staffs for the first time at reception, staging, onward movement, and integration (RSOI), they are behind the power curve.

> **Leader training program:** The TACP ALO, the lead planner, and the project officer from the supporting air force, as well as the AF unit, GLD, and BDE staff, must all be present in order to build that initial communication structure.

> **RSOI Day 3:** Joint fires integration brief/tabletop discussion at the Raven's Nest. BDE Staff (i.e., the BDE fire support officer) must be present at the joint fires integration brief.

5. Issue: The S-2 cell (intelligence) did not prepare the battlefield to achieve effective fires.

Discussion: S-2 cell was not able to find, fix, nor track targets prior to CAS coming on-station, which led to CAS not being effectively used. Additionally, the lack of a battle rhythm and time-correlated data lead to an inaccurate intelligence COP, which in turn led to poor fires integration in the targeting process.

Recommendation: The ALO and the intelligence, surveillance, and reconnaissance (ISR) liaison officer need to link-up with the BCT collection manager and S2 at home station to discuss capabilities of ISR assets, and develop contracts and/or procedures to effectively utilize those resources.

6. Issue: Integration of brigade staff

Discussion: Staff relationships did not develop at an effective level during rotation 18-02, leading to multiple challenges during the force-on-force

(FoF) phases. Planning processes at the beginning were very weak and there was no clear battle rhythm for planning. Intelligence collection was extremely poor, and the S2 officer seemed inexperienced throughout most of the rotation. This led to no clear intelligence picture, limited observations, lack of targets for CAS assets, and the inability to mass joint fires against the enemy. The BDE staff became very reactionary to the enemy's scheme of maneuver, instead of dictating the way the BDE wanted the battlefield to be shaped. In addition, a lack of planning led to a lack of a COP across the entire BCT. This lack of a COP led to a lack of execution of all warfighting functions during the FoF phases. Planning, integration, and building staff relationships is essential for success on the battlefield as well as during the fog of war.

Recommendation: BDE staff relationships must be built at home station before going to any training event, and more so before deploying. The air support operation squadron (ASOS) needs to have quarterly meetings with each element of the BDE staff in order to build up those relationships. Having these meetings will help strengthen the bond between the Air Force and the Army members, and stress the doctrinal importance of what each element brings to the fight.

7. Issue: Deep fight CAS effects

Discussion: The Army staff's guidance was to employ CAS in the deep fight, while the BDE's organic assets focused on the close fight. The BDE lacked a robust find, fix, track, target, engage, and assess (F2T2EA) process, often using CAS fighters to search for targets. Fighters performed a significant amount of NTISR for the preponderance of their on-station time. This directly resulted in CAS assets employing less than one third of all available ordnance.

Recommendation: The BDE must have an effective F2T2EA process in order for CAS to be successful in the deep fight. The S2 and ALO should improve on integrating the Joint Surveillance Target Attack Radar System (JSTARS) to support the BDE's triggers, named/targeted areas of interest and their scheme of maneuver within their battle space.

8. Issue: Airspace management

Discussion: Discussion between the BDE aviation element (BAE) and TACP about the use of joint airspace during the final exercise contracts brief during RSOI week was extremely poor. The BAE officer was reluctant to work with the TACP's fixed-wing stack plan, and set artificial and arbitrary constraints that hindered the airspace plan. Lacking airspace synchronization at the regiment inhibited warfighting functions to mass effective joint fires. Weak Army forces unit airspace plans also led to the lack of an effective observation plan with ISR assets in the airspace. Although the ISR planning sessions were well-developed, the execution was extremely poor. The sensor-to-shooter kill chain was highly inefficient during the execution phase, as the timeline was degraded and lacked information about a specific target. There was also no utilization of formal or informal airspace control authority (ACA), which could have greatly helped the execution of joint fires.

Recommendation: At home station, the regimental staff needs to work at all echelons to develop a strong airspace plan. If the staff spends more time together integrating, planning sessions will result in a well-developed and better airspace plan. The ASOS needs to stress what the fixed-wing stack plan for a fight will be, and how long fixed-wing assets will be on station. This cross communication flow will result in an effective use of joint fires against a near-peer threat.

9. Issue: CAS in a contested environment

Discussion: During Rotation 18-03, the rotational BDE and fighter squadron struggled to deal with surface-to-air threats that specifically targeted fixed-wing aircraft. Three aircraft (one unmanned aircraft system [UAS] and two F-16s) received high probability of kill shots from the real world SA-6 and SA-8 emitters. There were times when the rotational fighter squadron did not have accurate situational awareness on where the threats were, and when they did, they were reluctant to conduct CAS even when the targets were outside the missile engagement area (MEZ).

Recommendation: The BDE needs to understand the impact of surface-to-air threats on aircraft that are operating in their area of operations. Rotational fighter/bomber squadrons need to know where the threats are and still strike targets if they fall outside the MEZ, or if the artillery locating radar (ALR) is high enough to justify the attack. If the threat cannot be mitigated by avoiding it, the threat will have to be suppressed or killed (using the avoid, suppress, or kill method). This will require the use of electronic attack, artillery suppression, destructive direct fires, aerial delivered munitions, or a combination of these.

B. Executive Summary of 18-03 Fire Support After Action Report (AAR)

Issues:

1. The amount of ordnance that AF aircraft brought back was more than expected (a large portion was not utilized).

2. The ability of the BDE to find valid targets for aircraft and artillery to strike.

3. The ability of the BDE to clear the ground prior to employment of air-to-surface and surface-to-surface fires.

Discussion: During 18-03, the BDE only employed approximately one third of the ordnance that was brought to the fight by the rotational fighter squadron and MQ-9s. The primary reason for this was that the BDE struggled with finding valid targets for the aircraft to strike. With no valid targets to strike upon check-in, aircraft were tasked with conducting NTISR or reconnaissance, and had to find their own targets to strike. The BDE improved on this after the joint fires AAR, but the amount of ordnance that the BDE utilized increased only slightly. The ability of the BDE to quickly clear the ground for all forms of fires slowed down this process. From observations as a GFW staff, the information that was passed from the ground to the air players was accurate in regards to the forward line of own troops (FLOT), but there was second guessing on the part of all parties on he accuracy of that information. The double and triple checking of this information by all parties slowed down employment, and resulted in fewer targets being struck.

Recommendation: The BDE fire support coordinator tasked the BDE fire support officer to work with the BDE S2 and determine how the BDE conducts targeting for all fires. Targeting meeting working groups are occurring, and most of the key players are present, but the outputs and the transfer of working groups from future to current operations is still not happening rapidly enough for the major combat operations (MCO) fight against a near-peer adversary. The BDE will continue to work on how they utilize their forward observers, joint fires observers, remotely piloted aircraft systems, radars, etc. This is a reoccurring trend throughout all BDEs within the National Training Center.

C. Green Flag-West

1. Issue: BDE/BN Battle Tracking of Blue vs. Red Forces

Discussion: The 5th ASOS was not able to efficiently and consistently battle track friendly and enemy locations. BDE and BN staff's poor battle tracking of the current location of friendly forces made it difficult to employ CAS in a reasonable time. Also, poor communication and network connectivity among the TACP echelons made it difficult to cross check coordinates of nearby friendly units. The lack of fire support coordination measures (FSCMs), BN boundaries, and clearly defined adjoining area of operations hampered any geographical deconfliction. As a result, a significant amount of allocated CAS aircraft spent their time looking at friendly locations and performing the NTISR role.

Recommendation: ALO/TACP staff need to advocate to the BDE/BN staff for the control measures required (e.g., FSCMs, BN boundaries, and clearly defined adjoining area of operations) in order to safely and effectively employ CAS, and minimize the risk of fratricide.

2. Issue: The observation plan was limited, and did not allow for a prompt sensor-to-shooter timeline in execution.

Discussion: Army staff was heavily reliant on UASs when building their observation plan, and did not incorporate observation points or forward observers as a tiered plan. Therefore, when weather and poor visibility prevented UAS use, the Army staff and TACP were unable to source CAS targets. Aircraft during those times did not have a clear task or purpose, and were unable to perform their primary CAS mission, and instead preformed NTISR. The non-doctrinal use of CAS in the MCO flight might take away combat power from another ground commander who is also in need of CAS.

Recommendation: ALOs, noncommissioned officers in charge (NCOICs), and battalion air liaison officers (BALOs) need to educate their Army staff on how to properly integrate CAS into their scheme of maneuvers during the MCO critical and decisive points. Continuing education and increased understanding on the proper CAS use will enable TACPs to achieve the ground commander's intent.

3. Issue: Historically, ASOSs have struggled to reliably communicate among echelons using high frequency as their only beyond line-of-sight (BLOS) communication means, and also limited their primary, alternate, contingency, and emergency (PACE) plan

Discussion: As ASOSs continue to prepare for the NTC and/or deployment, they need to keep in mind the correct communication security (COMSEC) titles to request from the S6, the correct radio firmware versions required, and the COMSEC turnover dates in order for the successful implementation of 25K integrated waveform (IW) satellite communications (SATCOM) (25K IW SATCOM).

Recommendation: Take advantage of the home station 25K IW SATCOM training program and equipment familiarization exercise prior to deploying. 5th ASOS was the first ASOS in Green Flag-West to successfully use 25K IW SATCOM as the joint air request net (JARN) with the air support operations center. The inability to successfully use the allocated 25K IW SATCOM channel for BLOS communication has been a trend among previous ASOS units. The 5th ASOS home station training, preparation, and testing of 25K IW SATCOM procedures with the NTC ASOC, enabled its successful use of a BLOS means of communication, other than high frequency.

AIRSPACE MANAGEMENT SYSTEM

The BCD airspace management section works to ensure the safe and efficient use of airspace. The key to this effort is the integration of all ARFOR airspace consumers into the airspace control plan. Airspace management represents ARFOR equities in the development of the airspace control plan, ensuring that Army assets are enabled, and not encumbered, by the plan. The BCD airspace management section links directly into the air operations center (AOC) airspace management team (AMT) to provide ARFOR inputs, and receive the airspace control order (ACO).

Airspace management supports both plans and operations sections within the BCD. Although all personnel in the airspace management section are trained to perform both plans and operations roles, they remain distinct skill sets. Key tasks performed to support operations include dynamic airspace deconfliction, implementing updates to the ARFOR unit airspace plans, and disseminating the ACO to ARFOR units. Key tasks that airspace management execute in support of plans include shaping and disseminating the airspace control plan, reviewing and vetting ARFOR unit airspace plans, and sending the ARFOR friendly order of battle to the AOC AMT.

Key Airspace Lessons Learned and Tactics, Techniques, and Procedures:

1. Issue: Airspace control plan (ACP)

Discussion: The ACP is the rulebook for airspace consumers in a joint environment. As such, it is vital that ARFOR has input to the ACP, as well as understanding of the ACP.

Recommendation: A poorly designed or poorly understood ACP creates massive inefficiencies for the airspace management section. The upfront effort of bringing ARFOR elements into the ACP discussion early is well worth the payout during execution of the ACP. It is vital that ARFOR understands their roles and responsibilities within the ACP.

2. Issue: Joint air-ground integration cells

Discussion: Joint air-ground integration cells (JAGICs) are a TTP that enable enhanced mission command within division-and-corps-level echelons; however JAGICs sometimes fail to abide by ACP requirements and create friction between ARFOR and joint airspace users.

Recommendation: The airspace management section must ensure that ARFOR keeps subordinate JAGICs within the limits of their authorities. Although JAGICs are given considerable freedom to conduct operations within their area of operations, the airspace control authority (ACA) may revoke such authorities if there is doubt in their abilities to control airspace safely and efficiently.

3. Issue: Authorities

Discussion: One of the most vital services the BCD provides to the ARFOR is the clarification of authorities between joint components. BCD airspace management must convey to ARFOR units the authorities that have been delegated to them, and their obligations to maintain those authorities.

Recommendation: Problems with authorities frequently center on the JAGIC TTP. It is crucial that airspace management educates subordinate ARFOR units on their obligations in regards to airspace control, unit airspace plans, and other requirements that the ACA mandates.

Real World Operations[2]

Over the past couple of years, the 5th BCD has made great strides to better emphasize and integrate airspace management into planning and execution phases of operations at all echelons. These successful efforts were locally recognized and lauded by I Corps and 25th Infantry Division leadership for increasing their staff's knowledge on joint airspace structure, and its impact on joint fires. This resulted in a greater efficiency and effectiveness in the employment of joint fires, which contributed to a very successful experience during the 25th Infantry Division Warfighter 17-04 event. If the U.S. Army is to maximize effectiveness in an increasingly complex operating environment, airspace planning and execution must transition from deconfliction and synchronization to synthesis. The 5th BCD attests their successful contributions of movement in this direction to the following:

1) Integration of 5th BCD airspace personnel into daily air operations center operations

The 5th BCD coordinated to integrate airspace personnel with the 613rd AOC to conduct daily airspace operations supporting both real-world training missions and exercises. They received briefings on Air Force mission command systems, ACO development, and coordination with necessary entities and sections within the AOC. This provides the following:

- Indoctrinates and prepares newly assigned personnel on roles and responsibilities of the AOC and 5th BCD.

- Provides 5th BCD airspace personnel practical exposure on the functionality of the Theater Battle Management Core System (TBMCS) and its interoperability with the Tactical Airspace Integration System (TAIS).

- Allows a better understanding of processes within the AOC, which can be used to better facilitate and integrate the needs of the land component commander (LCC) during exercises.

2) Facilitation of quarterly multiservice airspace working groups for land component airspace echelons

In 2017, the 5th BCD began hosting quarterly multiservice airspace working groups with I Corps; 25th Infantry Division; United States Army, Pacific Command (USARPAC); Army Joint Support Team (AJST); and local brigades within Hawaii, which are still ongoing. These airspace working groups have provided a forum for leaders, planners, and operators to discuss key joint airspace planning and execution topics and issues. Attendees can join in-person, telephonically, or by video teleconference. Attendees can include:

- 1st Air Support Operations Squadron, I Corps G3 airspace, fires, and collection management sections

- 17th Field Artillery Brigade

- 25th Combat Aviation Brigade (CAB) and 25th Division Artillery (DIVARTY) representatives

- 25th Infantry Division G6 network

- USARPAC G3 aviation personnel

- 613th AOC airspace personnel

- Army Joint Support Team

Some previous topics/issues discussed at the airspace working groups are:

- Introduction to AOC operations

- Efficiently planning and clearing ground fires above the coordination altitude

- Achieving network interoperability between Air Force and Army mission command systems

- Processing and submittal of air support requests

- Kill box and strike coordination and reconnaissance operations

- Planned and dynamic airspace requests beyond the fire support coordination line (FSCL)

- Proper UAP submittal from the LCC to air component commander (ACC)

3) Collaborative doctrine, operations, and equipment training with local airspace organizations

The 5th BCD collaborates locally with the 25th Infantry Division G3 Aviation to provide airspace managers and operators with training on doctrine, operations, and equipment. Attendees include the 5th BCD, 25th Infantry Division, 25th CAB, 25th DIVARTY, 2nd Infantry Brigade and 3rd Infantry Brigade Combat Team (IBCT), and 3rd IBCT personnel, and is also extended to USARPAC, Mission Training Complex (MTC), and 303rd Maneuver Enhancement Brigade (MEB).

The week-long training is conducted annually, and focuses on the following topics:

- Airspace clearance procedures
- UAP development
- TAIS personalization, functionality, and maintenance
- Annex development

DOTMLPF-P Descriptions

Refer to pages 43 through 47 for specific the DOTMLPF-P descriptions and implications. All DOTMLPF-P information on those pages is identical, except for Training, which includes:

3rd BCD Korea (BCD-K) Major Training Events

Ulchi Freedom Guardian and Key Resolve are the two major joint service, multi-component, multinational, peninsula-wide exercises 3rd BCD-K use to execute wartime proficiencies and validate mission essential task readiness. These events require extensive planning leading up to the exercise, and multiple subsequent planning cycles throughout. Training objectives are relatively consistent; however, the objectives are revisited during every exercise that is similar to the evolving operational environment in the Korean theater of operation (KTO). The two primary phases of these exercises focus on posturing for hostilities/initial phases of conflict, and the possible event that friendly forces are required to execute an offensive.

Endnotes:

1. Arrol, Matthew R., LTC, FA, Deputy Commanding Officer, 19th Battlefield Coordination Detachment, "Observations."

2. Ibid.

APPENDIX A

Key Leader Interview

COL Samuel J. Saine

Assistant Commandant, U.S. Army Field Artillery School

1. What would you say are the five biggest issues that face battlefield coordination detachments (BCDs) today?

- Lack of a culminating training event (CTE)/WFX to train and assess BCDs as a collective team.

- The ability to conduct collective training (which requires the Joint Force Air Component Commander [JFACC] and staff, and the Joint Force Land Component Commander [JFLCC] and staff) outside of real-world operations. Training is lacking within large-scale ground combat operations (LSGCO) scenarios at the theater level to exercise BCDs.

- BCD manning is sub-optimal to fully support a JFLCC in LSGCO, especially when the BCD would likely support combined joint task force headquarters (CJTF HQ) if ground focused, given the lack of manning and roles of the Marine liaison officers and the special operations forces (SOF) special operations liaison element (SOLE).

- The ability to train and internally sustain forward central command, and rear.

- At Shaw Air Force Base (AFB), global commitments in 4th BCD and with expeditionary ground liaison officer (GLO)/ground liaison detachment (GLD) requirements in mission employment (ME).

- Lack of understanding in the Army of joint process, or the joint targeting cycle.

2. What training changes would you say are required, and where, in order to improve unit readiness to ensure Soldiers and leaders hit the ground running?

- Send all BCD-bound Soldiers on temporary duty (TDY) in-route to appropriate Joint/U.S. Air Force (USAF) training at Hurlburt Field AFB and Nellis AFB before signing into a BCD.

- Link a brigade (BDE) CTE/WFX to a corps WFX, ideally AOR focused.

- Place educated BCD members on joint process and operational level staff functions to better prepare them to operate within a JFACC or JFLCC staff.

- Assign personnel to the BCD who already have previous experience above the brigade combat team (BCT) level (field artillery brigade [FA BDE], division [DIV], corps) to reduce gaps in understanding.

- Create opportunities for future and assigned BCD members to attend Army training, on both air space and advanced Army Battle Command System (ABCS)/Army Mission Command System (AMCS).

3. What were your keys to success?

- Building and fostering relationships.

- Taking an approach of who all needs to know intelligence information, to ensure maximum collaboration.

- Building collective training opportunities to mature joint systems and exercises' collaborative processes across services, especially in targeting, intelligence operations, airspace, common operational picture (COP), and sustainment/logistics.

- Fully embedding and integrating BCD members into each division of the air operations center (AOC).

4. Based on your experience, what changes are required in our leader development and education system to better prepare leaders for the current operating environment?

- More joint education in the BCD and across the Army at the field grade level and above.

- Build a training and operational enterprise within the Army. Expand the Army Multi-Domain Targeting Center (AMTC).

- Educate the Army leaders on the joint targeting process.

- Expand the Army's operational fires capability (systems and staff capacity).

- Army organizations/HQ do not understand joint processes, or exercise them. When they shift to a joint or combined construct/environment, they continue to try to use Army processes (military decisionmaking process [MDMP]; decide, detect, deliver, and assess [D3A], etc.) and either cannot or will not grasp or use joint methods, hampering staffs.

5. When you handed over the reins to your replacement commander, what was the one significant lesson learned that you passed on?

- It is essential to use mission command in the execution of a mission both in the continental United States (CONUS), and across the CENTCOM AOR.

6. What were some of the greatest challenges you or your Soldiers faced?

- Systems integrations (ABCS and Theater Battle Management Core System [TBMCS]; COP; Joint Automated Deep Operations Coordination System [JADOCS]).

- Continuous Army Force Generation (ARFORGEN) cycle to man forward headquarters (FWD HQ) and forward ground liaison detachment locations.

7. What are some of the highlights, or the highlight, of your tour as a BCD Commander?

- Supporting the combined joint task force and other intelligence requirements operations

- Supporting Resolute Support

- Integration of a FA BDE team, and systems in the combined air operations center (CAOC), to enable delivery of rocket fires.

8. What do you feel is perhaps the greatest lesson learned regarding your unit's tactics, techniques, and procedures (TTP) that could be shared to benefit other units in the U.S. Army in general?

- Role of the GLO/GLD in execution of close air support (CAS).

- Role of BCD in LSGCO at the theater level.

- Central role of the JFACC in joint targeting, and the BCD's role within that for the JFLCC.

- Command relationship of the Army Air and Missile Defense Command (AAMDC) and the air defense artillery brigade (ADA BDE) assets with the USAF, versus with the U.S. Army.

APPENDIX B

Battlefield Coordination Detachment (BCD) World-Wide Locations/Mission
4th U.S. Army Active component, 2nd Information Operations Command Army National Guard

3RD BCD-KOREA (BCD-K) MISSION

The 3rd BCD-K represents the Geographic Combatant Commander (GCC) and the Commander, Army forces (ARFOR) to the Commander, Air Combat Command in the Korean air operations center (KAOC), in order to synchronize air power with the ground scheme of fires and maneuver within the Korean theater of operations (KTO).

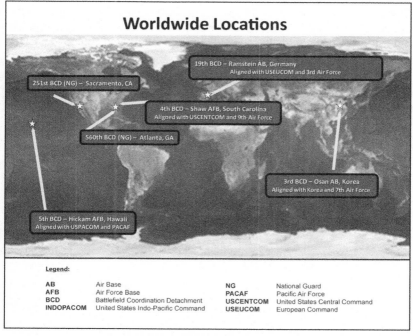

Figure B-1. BCD worldwide locations.

Command Relationship

Within the Korean Theater of Operations there are three commands, the United States Forces, Korea (USFK), the Combined Forces Command, Korea (CFC), and the United Nations Command (UNC).

All have a role in Armistice and in combat. Figure B-1 depicts a graphical depiction of the 3rd BCD relationships.

The BCD has relationships with several major commands, USFK, CFC, and UNC within the KTO. Those relationships change.

As the administrative control (ADCON) on a day-to-day basis, the 3rd BCD is considered a major subordinate command (MSC) under the Eighth Army (8A). The 8A Commander (CDR) has Uniform Code of Military Justice (UCMJ)/Court Martial convening authority and the 8A staff provides Service related support.

As the operational control (OPCON) to the Combined Joint Staff, Operations (CJ3) for real world operations and Combined Forces Command, Korea (CFC) lead exercises, the 3rd BCD wear the USFK patch and is a combined unit that supports the combined ground component CDR in the combined air operations center.

As stated in the mission, the 3rd BCD represent the GCC in the AOC during crisis and conflict. It has coordinating authority with the GCC primarily through the Republic of Korea (ROK) BCD. The 3rd BCD also maintains coordinating authority with the 7th Air Force (AF) CDR/Air Component CDR and USFK/UNC Deputy Commanding General.

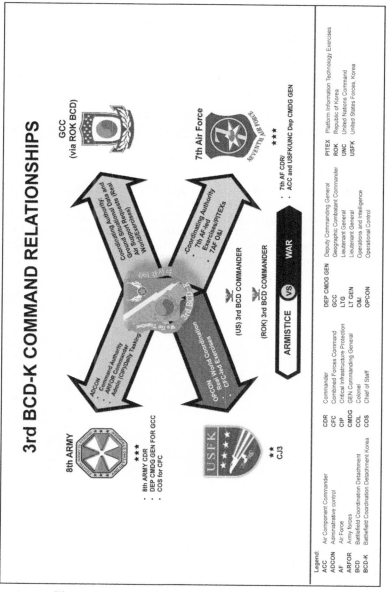

Figure B-2. 3rd BCD-K command relationships.

4TH BCD MISSION

The 4th BCD conducts liaison, integration, and coordination between the Combined Land Forces Component Commander and the Combined Forces Air Component Commander (CFACC) in support of land power requirements, and to synchronize air and ground operations within the U.S. Central Command (USCENTCOM) area of responsibility (AOR) and established combined-joint operating areas.

Note: The 4th BCD's mission is slightly different than the other BCDs. The 4th BCD maintains a permanent presence forward deployed in support of the USCENTCOM AOR.

5TH BCD MISSION

The 5th BCD liaisons from the Theater Joint Force Land Component Commander (JFLCC) (under the United States Army, Pacific Command [USARPAC]), and designated ARFOR CDRs, to the Theater Joint Force Air Component Commander (JFLCC) (under the Pacific Air Forces [PACAF]) to coordinate cross-domain activities to enable mission command and the synchronization of joint fires into unified land operations in the Pacific AOR.

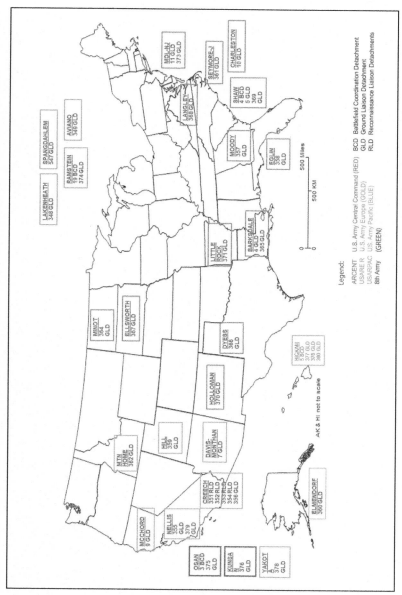

Figure B-3 across the globe.

APPENDIX C

Tactical Standard Operating Procedures (TACSOP) example

https://www.jllis.mil/?doit=view&disp=cdrview&cdrid=126661

Available to authorized CAC users only; account registration required.

APPENDIX D

Glossary

8A	Eighth Army
AAMDC	Army Air and Missile Defense Command
AAR	after action report
ABCS	Army Battle Command System
ACA	airspace control authority
ACC	Air Component Commander
ACM	airspace coordinating measure
ACMREQ	airspace control means request
ACO	airspace control order
ACP	airspace control plan
ADAM	air defense airspace management
ADCON	administrative control
ADRP	Army Doctrine Reference Publication
AF	Air Force
AFATDS	Advanced Field Artillery Tactical Data System
AFB	Air Force Base
AFLE	Air Force liaison element
AI	air interdiction
AIRCOM	air command
AJST	Army Joint Support Team
ALO	air liaison officer
ALR	artillery locating radar
AMCS	Army Mission Command System
AMD	air and missile defense
AMT	airspace management team
AMTC	Army Multi-Domain Targeting Center
AOC	air operations center
AOCC	air operation coordination center
AOD	air operations directive

AOR	area of responsibility
ARFOR	Army forces
ASCC	Army Service component command
ASOS	air support operations squadron
ASR	air support request
ATACMS	Army Tactical Missile System
ATD	advanced target development
ATO	air tasking order
ATP	Army Techniques Publication
BAE	brigade aviation element
BALO	battalion air liaison officer
BCD	battlefield coordination detachment
BCD-K	Battlefield Coordination Detachment-Korea
BCT	brigade combat team
BDE	brigade
BLOS	beyond line-of-sight
BN	battalion
C2	command and control
C4I	command, control, communication, computers, and intelligence
CAB	combat aviation brigade
CACC	combined analysis coordination center
CAOC	combined air operations center
CAS	close air support
C-BCD	combined battlefield coordination detachment
CBRNE	Chemical, Biological, Radiological, Nuclear, and Explosive
CCMD	combatant command
CDR	Commander
CENTCOM	Central Command
CFACC	Combined Force Air Component Commander
CFC	Combined Forces Command, Korea
CFLCC	Coalition Forces Land Component Commander

CIDNE	Combined Information Data Network Exchange
CJCS	Chairman of the Joint Chiefs of Staff
CJTCB	joint targeting coordination board
CJTF	combined joint task force
COD	combat operations division
COMARFOR	Commander, Army forces
COMSEC	communication security
CONPLAN	concept plan
CONUS	continental United States
COP	common operational picture
CPOF	Command Post of the Future
CTC	Combat Training Center
CTE	culminating training event
CUOPS	current operations
D3A	decide, detect, deliver, and assess
DE	directed energy
DF18	Dynamic Front 18
DIV	division
DIVARTY	Division Artillery
DOD	Department of Defense
DOTMLPF-P	doctrine, organization, training, materiel, leadership and education, personnel, facilities, and policy
EA	electronic attack
EM	electromagnetic
EMS	electromagnetic spectrum
EP	electronic protection
ES	electronic warfare support
EW	electronic warfare
EWDO	electronic warfare duty officer
F2T2EA	find, fix, track, target, engage and assess
FA	field artillery
FECC	fires and effects coordination cell
FG	field grade

FLOT	forward line of own troops
FM	Field Manual
FoF	force-on-force
FSCL	fire support coordination line
FSCM	fire support coordination measure
FSE	fire support element
FSO	fire support officer
G3	Assistant Chief of Staff, Operations
G-CAS	ground alert-close air support
GCC	Geographic Combatant Commander
GCCS-A	Global Command and Control System-Army
GCSS-A	Global Combat Support System-Army
GFW	Green Flag-West
G-INT	ground alert-interdiction
GLD	ground liaison detachment
GLO	ground liaison officer
GMLRS	Guided Multiple Launch Rocket System
GRG	gridded reference graphic
HIDACZ	high-density airspace control zone
HPT	high-payoff target
HQ	headquarters
HQDA	Headquarters, Department of the Army
ICC	integrated command and control
IFF	identification, friend or foe
IOC	Information Operations Command (Land)
IRIS	Immediate Response Information System
ISR	intelligence, surveillance, and reconnaissance
ISRD	intelligence, surveillance, and reconnaissance division
IT	information technology
IW	integrated waveform
JAAR	joint after action report

JADOCS	Joint Automatic Deep Operation Coordination System
JAGIC	joint air-ground integration center
JALIC	joint air land integration cell
JAOC	joint air operations center
JAOP	joint air operations plan
JARN	joint air request net
JCR	joint capabilities release
JET	joint expeditionary team
JFACC	Joint Force Air Component Commander
JFC	Joint Force Commander
JFLCC	Joint Force Land Component Commander
JIIM	joint interagency, intergovernmental, and multinational
JIPTL	joint integrated prioritized target list
JITD	joint intermediate target development
JOA	joint operation area
JOFEC	Joint Operational Fires and Effects Course
JP	Joint Publication
JSTARS	Joint Surveillance Target Attack Radar System
JTCB	joint targeting coordination board
JTF	joint task force
KAOC	Korean air operations center
KTO	Korean theater of operations
LCC	Land Component Commander
LSGCO	large-scale ground combat operations
MAAP	master air attack plan
MARLE	Marine liaison element
MARLO	Marine liaison officer
MCO	major combat operation
MCTP	Mission Command Training Program
MDMP	military decision making process
ME	mission employment

METL	mission-essential task list
MEZ	missile engagement zone
MI	military intelligence
MIRC	military intelligence readiness command
MLRS	Multiple Launch Rocket System
MOA	memorandum of agreement
MOS	military occupational specialty
MSC	major subordinate command
MTT	mobile training teams
NAI	named area of interest
NALE	naval and amphibious liaison element
NATO	North Atlantic Treaty Organization
NCO	noncommissioned officer
NCOIC	noncommissioned officer in charge
NIPRNET	Non-Classified Internet Protocol Router Network
NTC	National Training Center
NTISR	non-traditional intelligence, surveillance, and reconnaissance
OC/T	observer-controller/trainer
OIC	officer in charge
OPCON	operational control
OPLAN	operation plan
OPORD	operation order
OPTEMPO	operating tempo
PACAF	Pacific Air Forces
PACE	primary, alternate, contingency, and emergency
PMCS	preventive maintenance checks and services
PME	professional military education
RLD	reconnaissance liaison detachment
ROE	rules of engagement
ROK	Republic of Korea
RPAs	remotely piloted aircraft systems

RSOI	reception, staging, onward movement, and integration
RTU	remote thermal unit
SA	situational awareness
SADO	senior air defense officer
SATCOM	satellite communications
SCAR	strike coordination and reconnaissance
SIF	selective identification feature
SIG	Signal
SIPRNET	Secret Internet Protocol Router Network
SITREP	situation report
SOF	special operations forces
SOLE	special operations liaison element
SOP	standard operating procedure
SME	subject matter expert
SYSAD	system administrator
TACC	Tactical Air Coordination Center
TACOP	tactical operation
TACP	tactical air control party
TACSOP	tactical standard operating procedures
TAI	target area of interest
TAIS	Tactical Airspace Integration System
TBM	theater ballistic missile
TBMCS	Theater Battle Management Core System
TDY	temporary duty
TET	targeting effects team
TJFLCC	Theater Joint Force Land Component Commander
TMD	theater missile defense
TO&E	table of organization and equipment
TPFDD	time-phased force and deployment data
TSC	theater support command
TST	time-sensitive target
TTP	tactics, techniques, and procedures

UAP	unit airspace plan
UAS	unmanned aircraft system
UAV	unmanned aerial vehicle
UCMJ	Uniform Code of Military Justice
ULO	unified land operations
USAACE	United States Army Aviation Center of Excellence
USAF	United States Air Force
USAREUR	United States Army, European Command
USARPAC	United States Army, Pacific Command
USCENTCOM	United States Central Command
USFK	United States Forces, Korea
USINDOPACOM	United States Indo-Pacific Command
USMC	United States Marine Corps
USMTF	United States message text format
USN	United States Navy
USPACOM	United States Pacific Command
WARP	web-based access and retrieval port
WFX	warfighter exercise
X-CAS	air alert-close air support
X-INT	air alert-interdiction

TERMS

Battlefield coordination detachment (BCD): An Army liaison located in the air operations center that provides selected operational functions between the Army forces and the air component commander.[1]

Joint operations: A general term to describe military actions conducted by joint forces and those Service forces employed in specific command relationships with each other, which of themselves, do not establish joint forces.[2]

Special operations: Operations requiring unique modes of employment, tactical techniques, equipment and training often conducted in hostile, denied, or politically sensitive environments and characterized by one or more of the following: time sensitive, clandestine, low visibility, conducted with and/or through indigenous forces, requiring regional expertise, and/or a high degree of risk.[3]

Special operations forces (SOF): Those Active and Reserve Component forces of the Services designated by the Secretary of Defense and specifically organized, trained, and equipped to conduct and support special operations.[4]

Endnotes

1. Joint Publication (JP) 3-03, *Joint Interdiction,* 09 SEP 2016.

2. JP 3-0, *Joint Operations,* 17 JAN 2017, Incorporating Change 1, 22 OCT 2018.

3. JP 3-05, *Special Operations*, 16 JUL 2014.

4. Ibid.

APPENDIX E

MEMORANDUM OF AGREEMENT BETWEEN THE UNITED STATES ARMY AND THE UNITED STATES AIR FORCE FOR ARMY/AIR FORCE LIAISON SUPPORT

MEMORANDUM OF AGREEMENT

BETWEEN THE

UNITED STATES ARMY

AND THE

UNITED STATES AIR FORCE

FOR

ARMY/AIR FORCE LIAISON SUPPORT

31 March 2011

1. This document is a Service Memorandum of Agreement (MOA) for home station and deployed liaison support and supersedes the Memorandum of Agreement between the United States Army and the United States Air Force for Liaison Support, 23 January 2008. This MOA is consistent with and supports joint doctrine as described in Joint Pub 3-09.3, *Close Air Support,* dated 8 July 2009; Joint Pub 3-59, *Meteorological and Oceanographic Operations,* dated 24 September 2008; and Joint Pub 3-17, *Air Mobility Operations,* 2 October 2009. Specific references to close air support (CAS) and associated definitions are as referenced in the joint publication. The policies set forth in this agreement specifically provides for:

   a. Exchange of USA and USAF liaison personnel to support training and combat operations of USA and USAF units and headquarters, including guidance for the assignment and duties of liaison personnel; and

   b. Logistical and administrative support for USA and USAF liaison personnel assigned to sister Service installations; and

   c. Increasing the capabilities of USA and USAF personnel in training and combat operations.

2. This Service MOA has been staffed and agreed to by the above Services to provide common guidance for the assignment, duties, and support of Air Component Coordination Elements (ACCE), Air Liaison Officers (ALO), Air Mobility Liaison Officers (AMLO), Air Support Operations Centers (ASOC), Army Liaison Officers (LNO), Army Mobility Officers (AMO), Battalion Air Liaison Officers (BALO), Battlefield Coordination Detachments (BCD), Ground Liaison Detachments (GLD), Ground Liaison Officers (GLOs), Joint Fires Observers (JFO), Intelligence, Surveillance, and Reconnaissance Liaison Officers (ISRLO)/Non-Commissioned Officers (ISR NCO),

1

Reconnaissance Liaison Officers (RLO), Space Liaison Officers and NCOs, Tactical Air Control Parties (TACPs), and TACP Joint Terminal Attack Controllers (JTAC) supporting Air Force and Army organizations.

3. The Services will implement this agreement upon signature by the CSA and CSAF or designated approval authority and will review it every two years on the anniversary of the current agreement. Review will be initiated alternately between the Department of the Army and Headquarters United States Air Force (first review after signing). In the event more than two years passes without review, either Service may initiate a review.

2

I. PURPOSE.

The purpose of this MOA is to provide Service guidance to USA and USAF Major Commands for liaison duties during home station training, collective training and deployed operations. The provisions of this document are applicable to all Air Component Coordination Elements (ACCE), Air Liaison Officers (ALO), Air Mobility Liaison Officers (AMLO), Air Support Operations Centers (ASOC), Army Liaisons Officer (LNO), Army Mobility Officers (AMO), Battalion Air Liaison Officers (BALO), Battlefield Coordination Detachments (BCD), Ground Liaison Detachments (GLD), Ground Liaison Officers (GLO), ISRLO/ISRNCO, Joint Fires Observers (JFO), Reconnaissance Liaison Officers (RLO), Space Liaison Officers/NCOs, Tactical Air Control Parties (TACP), and TACP Joint Terminal Attack Controllers (JTAC).

II. BACKGROUND.

The current Air-to-Ground support structure is based upon the CSAF/CSA 1965 Agreement, "Concept for Improved Air - Ground Coordination." This MOA updates the "Memorandum of Agreement between the United States Army and the United States Air Force for Liaison Support" (23 January 2008), and captures changes in doctrine and agreements between the Services since the signing of that document. The USAF provides weather support to the Army based upon an inter-service support agreement first signed in 1949. The current Army weather support structure and the provisions of this support are provided in Army Regulation (AR) 115-10/Air Force Instruction (AFI) 15-157 (Interservice Publication (IP) 15-157 *Weather Support for the U.S. Army.*"

III. SCOPE.

The basic provisions of this Agreement apply to all USA and USAF Major Commands and remain in effect following partial or full mobilization.

IV. OBJECTIVE.

The objective of this Agreement is to increase the joint capabilities; identify joint interdependencies; and standardize air-ground training, equipment interoperability, and combat operations of the USA and USAF.

V. PROVISIONS.

A. Subject to the authority of the combatant commander, the USAF will provide:

1. An ACCE to an Army organization, as required, when it serves as the Joint Force Land Component Commander (JFLCC) or, as a joint task force (JTF). The ACCE is the direct representative of the Commander, Air Force Forces (COMAFFOR)/Joint Force Air Component Command (JFACC) and coordinates with the JFLCC staff-in either a supporting or supported role. When the Joint Force Commander (JFC) does not establish Joint Force Functional Components, the COMAFFOR will provide an ACCE to the Commander, Army Forces (COMARFOR). The ACCEs will participate in training

3

events and exercises for Army Service Component Commands (ASCC) and for COMARFOR staffs designated for operational deployment to maintain combat mission readiness. In the event that full unit participation is not feasible, the Air Force will provide an exercise cell for required functionality.

2. A Modular ASOC in Direct Support to the Army tactical command echelons (e.g., division and/or corps), as the focal point for supporting air operations. As a direct subordinate of the Air and Space Operations Center (AOC), the ASOC is responsible for the direction and control of air operations directly supporting the ground combat element. The ASOCs will be habitually aligned to each of the 10 active duty divisions once fully operationally capable (FY15 projected) to develop the teamwork needed to maintain combat readiness.

3. Officers to act as liaisons to U.S. Army Forces Command (FORSCOM), U.S. Army Training and Doctrine Command (TRADOC). These officers will provide liaison with the appropriate USAF MAJCOM and special staff assistance to the Army organization commander.

4. The ALOs to Army corps, division, and brigade to provide liaison and special staff assistance to the ground unit commander. The ALOs will participate in all appropriate training events and operations of the supported organization. The U.S. Army echelons will incorporate ALO collective and individual training requirements into their overall training plans. Brigade ALOs will establish liaison with the Brigade JFO manager to coordinate concurrent JFO, JTAC, and Forward Air Controller (Airborne) (FAC(A)) CAS training where possible. This liaison will be established in the brigades to which the ASOS provides an ALO.

5. The BALOs will be an experienced noncommissioned officer (E-6 or higher) or officer habitually aligned with a maneuver battalion (defined in paragraph V.A.6.). The BALOs will participate in appropriate training events and operations of the supported battalion. The U.S. Army echelons will incorporate BALO collective and individual training requirements into their overall training plans.

6. A TACP in Direct Support to each U.S. Army corps, division, brigade combat team (BCT), and each BCT maneuver battalion for liaison and to provide terminal attack control of CAS missions. These TACPs will have a minimum of two JTACs for each corps, division, brigade combat team, and maneuver battalion. For the purpose of this MOA, maneuver battalions in the BCT include Infantry Battalions, Stryker Infantry Battalions, Combined Arms Battalions, and Reconnaissance Squadrons. There is also a requirement for the Air Force to provide JTACs at the maneuver company/troop level of these battalions/squadrons. The Air Force will provide a Terminal Attack Control Team with a minimum of one JTAC for each maneuver company/troop level in the available pool and that portion of the ready pool identified for deployment. Support Brigades may receive JTACs on a case by case basis dependent on their mission. The TACPs include ALOs/BALOs, enlisted technicians capable of planning and integrating air support into ground combat operations, and qualified JTACs to execute those operations. Depending on the echelon supported, the TACP may be augmented by Air Force Intelligence, Space,

4

or other Subject Matter Experts as required to meet Joint Force Commander objectives. The TACPs will be habitually aligned with their supported Army unit to develop the teamwork needed to maintain combat readiness. The U.S. Army echelons will incorporate TACP collective and individual training requirements into their overall training plans.

7. The USAF provides the Army weather support in accordance with AR 115-10/AFI 15-157 (IP), *Weather Support for the U.S. Army*.

8. The AMLOs to liaison elements at Army corps, division, theater sustainment commands, separate regiment, selected brigade echelons, and other jointly validated headquarters to provide air mobility liaison and special staff assistance to the ground commander. The AMLOs will participate in all appropriate training events and operations of the supported organization. The U.S. Army echelons will incorporate AMLO collective and individual training requirements into their overall training plans.

9. The AF/ISR to liaison elements at Army corps, division, and other jointly validated headquarters to provide AF/ISR capabilities/limitations and special staff assistance to the ground commander. The U.S. Army echelons will incorporate AF/ISR training requirements into their overall training plans.

10. The AF/Electronic Warfare Officers (EWO): Tactical and operational electronic warfare (EW) integration including planning, execution and assessment will be conducted between Army Division and Brigade EWOs and AF EWOs serving in EW Coordination Cells at the Corps/Division and EW Elements at the Brigade level. The Air Force and Army EWOs will work jointly through the EW Integrated Reprogramming (EWIR) process for the reprogramming of EW assets such as aircraft and rotary wing self-defense systems, warning receivers, and counter-improvise explosive devices EW (CREW) systems.

B. Subject to the authority of the combatant commander, the U.S. Army will provide:

1. A BCD as liaison to the AOC and/or to the component designated by the joint force commander to plan, coordinate, and deconflict air operations. The BCD will integrate U.S. Army operational requirements into the air tasking order development process. The BCDs will be assigned to the ASCC with duty at each Numbered Air Force supporting a geographic combatant command: 1AF (AFNORTH), 3AF (AFEUR), 7AF (AFKOR), USAFCENT, 12AF (AFSOUTH), and 13AF (AFPAC). The BCD functions for 1AF and for 17AF will be tailored liaisons, based upon the nature of the NAF's missions. The ASCC will provide an Army LNO to the respective Numbered Air Force staff. The BCDs will participate in training events and exercises with the above Numbered Air Forces or USAF organizations designated to perform the above planning and coordinating functions in an operational deployment to maintain combat mission readiness. In the event that full unit participation is not feasible, the Army will provide an exercise cell for required functionality. The U.S. Air Force echelons will incorporate BCD collective and individual training requirements into their overall training plans.

5

2. Army LNO to Numbered Air Forces, and other major AF organizations based upon jointly agreed to requirements. These LNOs will provide liaison with appropriate Army organizations and special staff assistance to the Air Force commander. The LNOs will be assigned to the appropriate Army organization with duty at the supported Air Force headquarters. The LNOs will participate in all training events for and operations of the supported organization.

3. Ground Liaison Detachments (GLD) assigned to each BCD with duty at all operational fighter wings, bomber wings, and airlift wings, reconnaissance squadrons, and Distributed Common Ground System sites (DCGS) with the exception of 7AF DGCS, in order to provide liaison and special staff assistance to the aligned Air Force Commander. Each GLD will include an active duty GLO, AMO, or RLO, and a noncommissioned officer with appropriate military operational specialties for the organization for which they provide support. The Reconnaissance Liaison Detachment (RLD) will be located at the sensor operator (mission pilot) location. Each GLD will train and deploy with its supported unit according to USA Commands' and USAF MAJCOMs' agreed upon requirements and priorities. The U.S. Air Force wings and squadrons will incorporate GLD/RLD collective and individual training requirements into their overall training plans.

C. The JFOs increase the capability of CAS employment for the ground force commander by extending CAS capability. They improve the capability to provide timely and accurate targeting data to JTACs and FAC (A) and perform autonomous terminal guidance operations. The BCT commanders are responsible for JFO program oversight. The Brigade JFO manager will establish active liaison and coordination with the Brigade ALO to include JFO/JTAC integration in their overall training plans. The goal is concurrent JFO, JTAC and FAC (A) CAS training, where possible.

D. The Army and Air Force recognize the importance of appropriate education and training for joint air ground operations. The liaisons described in this MOA will be school-trained, if there is an established course, so as to provide an effective interface between the Services. The Army and Air Force will seek opportunities to jointly develop doctrine and tactics, techniques and procedures (TTPs) through exchange of personnel between Service schools.

E. The supported unit will provide operational, logistical, maintenance, base operating support, contracting, and administrative support for ACCEs, AMLOs, ASOCs, BCDs, GLDs, and TACPs in accordance with Department of Defense directives, Service directives and Service agreements. Supported Army units will provide dedicated specialized vehicles of comparable mobility and survivability with crews, including armored personnel carriers, Stryker vehicles, and future Army manned ground vehicles as required with primary purpose to support aligned commander's air ground integration requirements.

F. Each Service will develop an ongoing, formal process to identify and address equipment interoperability issues. Every effort will be made to resolve issues at the lowest possible level. The scope of the process will address issues ranging from

6

equipment acquisition and modification, through fielding and deployment plans, to crypto key updates. When either Service modifies existing equipment, the other Service will be given as much advance notification as possible.

VI. IMPLEMENTATION.

Department of the Army and HQ USAF will publish policy and guidance to Major Commands for implementing this Agreement. Major Command commanders are authorized to publish command-level joint agreements and regulations to further define operational, logistical, maintenance and administrative support requirements and responsibilities. The AR 115-10/AFI 15-157 (IP) meets this intent for combat weather operations personnel and support. Unresolved issues will be elevated to the offices of primary responsibility of this Agreement for resolution.

FOR U.S. ARMY: FOR U.S. AIR FORCE:

GEORGE W. CASEY, JR.   NORTON A. SCHWARTZ
General, USA   General, USAF
Chief of Staff   Chief of Staff

OFFICES OF PRIMARY RESPONSIBILITY:

HQDA, DCS G-3/5/7   HQ USAF/A3/5

7

89

APPENDIX
TERMS OF REFERENCE.

Terms in this MOA are defined in Joint Pub 1-02, *Department of Defense Dictionary of Military and Associated Terms*, Joint Pub 3-09.3, *Close Air Support.*" The following terms are defined in this MOA:

A. Army Liaison Officer (LNO): The Army LNO will provide liaison between Army forces and component command headquarters and Numbered Air Forces (NAF). Normally an Army LNO is a combat arms field grade officer working with component command headquarters, and NAFs that do not have a Falconer AOC but still plans and execute joint operations or training (Army draft term/definition: Has not been approved as a Joint term).

B. Ground Liaison Detachment (GLD): Army personnel who support USAF fighter, bomber wings, and airlift wings, reconnaissance squadrons and DCGS sites. They advise air commanders primarily on Army organizations, operations, tactics, capabilities and coordinate with Army units during Joint operations. A GLD normally consists of one combat arms officer and one fire support NCO (13F40) (Army Draft term/definition: Has not been approved as a Joint term).

C. Habitual alignment. A documented standing support relationship between two organizations, or personnel and an organization.

D. ISR Liaison Officer (ISRLO). An ISRLO/NCO is an Air Force intelligence professional augmenting the Army at Corps, Division, and BCT when needed to facilitate collection management planning and execution. The ISRLOs assist the Army to understand National and Air Force ISR intelligence products, e.g., how to synchronize and integrate ISR into land component operations, product tasking, collection, processing, exploitation, and dissemination (TCPED) procedures, and techniques for rapid ISR support requests. This is particularly important as the predominant need for ISR grows during Irregular Warfare (IW) operations with a focus on counterinsurgency (COIN) and improvised explosive device (IED) network and device defeat.

8

COMBINED ARMS CENTER (CAC)
Additional Publications and Resources

The CAC home page address is: **https://usacac.army.mil**

Center for the Army Profession and Leadership (CAPL)
CAPL serves as the proponent for the Army Profession, Leadership, and Leader Development programs and assists the Combined Arms Center in the integration and synchronization of cross-branch, career management field, and functional area initiatives. CAPL conducts studies on the Army Profession, Leadership and Leader Development and produces publications, doctrine, programs and products that support current operations and drive change.

Combat Studies Institute (CSI)
CSI is a military history think tank that produces timely and relevant military history and contemporary operational history.

Combined Arms Doctrine Directorate (CADD)
CADD develops, writes, and updates Army doctrine at the corps and division level. Find doctrinal publications at either the Army Publishing Directorate (APD) or the Central Army Registry.

Foreign Military Studies Office (FMSO)
FMSO is a research and analysis center on Fort Leavenworth under the TRADOC G-2. FMSO manages and conducts analytical programs focused on emerging and asymmetric threats, regional military and security developments, and other issues that define evolving operational environments around the world.

Military Review (MR)
MR is a revered journal that provides a forum for original thought and debate on the art and science of land warfare and other issues of current interest to the U.S. Army and the Department of Defense.

TRADOC Intelligence Support Activity (TRISA)
TRISA is a field agency of the TRADOC G-2 and a tenant organization on Fort Leavenworth. TRISA is responsible for the development of intelligence products to support the policy-making, training, combat development, models, and simulations arenas.

Capability Development Integration Directorate (CDID)
CDID conducts analysis, experimentation, and integration to identify future requirements and manage current capabilities that enable the Army, as part of the Joint Force, to exercise Mission Command and to operationalize the Human Dimension.

Joint Center for International Security Force Assistance (JCISFA)
JCISFA's mission is to capture and analyze security force assistance (SFA) lessons from contemporary operations to advise combatant commands and military departments on appropriate doctrine; practices; and proven tactics, techniques, and procedures (TTP) to prepare for and conduct SFA missions efficiently. JCISFA was created to institutionalize SFA across DOD and serve as the DOD SFA Center of Excellence.

Support CAC in the exchange of information by telling us about your successes so they may be shared and become Army successes.